Copyright

i

Dedication

To my beautiful and beloved Cami.

Thank you for blessing my life beyond my wildest dreams.

Remember to pray and love yourself first.

Mummy is always with you.

About the Au

Nancy Elliott is an award-winning writer, an accredited Psychotherapist of 10 years, author, and Speaker. She is a leading single women's influencer specializing in all things to do with Love and relationships. Nancy is a high-performing 1-1 coach offering programs ranging from 3 months to 1 year and has been in private practice for many years. She is a mentor to women from all over the world, providing them with tools and techniques to get the Love they want.

Nancy's childhood was shaped by three generations of women who struggled with a lack of self-love, low self-worth, and codependency. Nancy inherited these traits and had her own struggles with self-love and relationships.

Determined to break this cycle, Nancy underwent many years of academic and self-study. She also gained immeasurable knowledge from her private practice helping women evolve beyond painful attachments patterns and issues of low self-worth.

Nancy created tools and techniques drawn from her clinical, theoretical and experiential knowledge. This dramatically enhanced her life and the life of her clients.

FOREWORD

These days, with the rise of reality TV, plastic surgery, Instagram filters, and online dating, the ideal love is infused with anxieties about our value, self-worth, sex and desire.

I hope to challenge popular, often unspoken assumptions about what constitutes meaningful love, and relationships by creating a paradigm shift around how we relate to ourselves and others from a therapeutic and spiritual core.

Notwithstanding the superficiality of social media and the increasing drive towards cultural materialism and separation, I see a lot of love in our world.

I hope to contribute to the studied and incisive efforts already taking place to redefine how we give and receive love, and how we work with it. Traditional psychotherapy traces back to childhood to find healing and transformation for the patient.

Today, leading-edge therapists understand that it is not as helpful as we once thought to keep going back and analysing the past; we can re-traumatise ourselves that way. Instead, we look forward to a desired future self and work backwards from there. I also emphasized having fun as we heal and deepen self-love. Otherwise, what's the point!

Love is our creator's greatest gift to us. It should be sacred, redemptive and healing for the individuals. The work is to love each other on a constant quest towards moving away from fear, insecurity and narcissism born out of developmental, historical and cultural trauma.

At this point, we are a traumatised world, and we need to heal. If we can acquire the tools, knowledge and courage to correct the way we give and receive love to ourselves and others. We can change the world—one person at a time.

This is my hope and prayer for me, you, and our world.

Nancy Elliott

London, England

Contents

The Ten Commandments of Love..

1. Thou shall admit when there is a problem in thine relationship

2. Thou shall not slip into denial nor into the DMs of others, but instead confront thou, thine own issues

3. Thou shall become EDUCATED on how to build safe and healthy attachments

4. Thou shall get help to release unresolved childhood trauma

5. Thou shalt not pretend it is all thine partners fault when it is not

6. Thou shalt expect commitment, as thou is worthy

7. Thou shalt not cuss, shut down or make a run for it when love gets hard

8. Thou shall NEVER judge thy friend's relationship struggles, and if can't say anything nice, thou keep thine mouth shut

9. Thou shalt pray and meditate daily, to regulate thine autonomic nervous System

10. Thou shall put thy First attention on thine OWN healing and wellbeing, but ALWAYS, and I mean ALWAYS keep it sexy.

Step 1

POWERLESSNESS

Recovering power and self-love
in you relationships

PART 1

With over a decade in a 12 step programme and a string of failed relationships under my belt, no children in sight, and fast approaching my late 30s, I realised something had to give.

I had to admit there was a problem in my romantic relationships - that they were the source of overwhelming pain, insecurity and confusion- and I was constantly losing myself in them.

In this chapter, we see how admitting there is a problem with our relationships, is the first step on the road to recovering our relationship health. *First is the health of our relationship* with ourselves and *second,* our relationships with others.

We want love, sure we do - *everybody* wants love - and we *shall* have it, but we want *good* love. Healthy communicative intimate and mutual love.

First, we need to figure out why it has not been working.

This week you will learn that Self-love is the answer to all your relationship problems. And you need to know this because your relationships will be nothing less than co-

Week 1

Welcome to the 12 Steps of the Single Girls Rehab Program. This week initiates your romantic relationship recovery.

In week one we admit that we lose power in our relationships and come to understand that self-love is the answer to all our relationship problems.

My use of tips, quotes, and songs aim at imbuing you with a spirit of fortitude, allowing you to traverse your inner terrain, with deeper self-love, wisdom and power.

I hope the vulnerability and honesty in the examples from my own childhood & failed relationships, will establish a sense of trust between us and enable you to risk exploring your past relationships without fear and shame.

We can get discouraged when remembering who hurt us, what happened, and how hard it was. Start this week envisaging a future self who is secure in her relationships and has evolved beyond unhealthy patterns in love.

After all, if I can transform my relationships beyond recognition, so can you, girl!

Now take a deep breath, channel Mariah Carey, and repeat after me three times:.

"There can be miracles, if you believe."

dependent without self-love—mic drop. Now, if this resonates, read on.

Being in a relationship, for some women, means abandoning herself and giving away a disproportionate amount of time and attention to the man in her life. I was one of these women.

As if this wasn't a problem enough for me, I was needy, insecure, and jealous. I genuinely believed it was my man's responsibility to make me happy. I mean, what else was he here for?

To my credit, I knew not to show that side of me too early. I mean, you don't lead with that. Right?

So, here I am, a relatively successful, confident, attractive, and ambitious woman in a relationship, and this is what I looked like.

I'm firing at 40 per cent of my capacity in all areas of my life. That's because I was *always* preoccupied with the man *du jour*. I just couldn't seem to hold on to myself and priorities.

For example, suppose I was on a work call, or on the phone with a distressed girlfriend or the doctor, or almost anyone and his number should suddenly flash up on my phone. In that case, I immediately have an adrenaline rush, and I'm like, to whoever it is on the other end of the phone. "Err, can I call you right back? I just *need* to take this call."

Work can wait; girlfriends can wait. *Everything* can wait. But *he* could not! That kind of priority problem.

So, on the one hand, quite a bad case of the codependencies. On the other, I'm fiercely independent, got my own shit, and have an unusually low tolerance for the ups and downs that naturally occur in any relationship.

This dizzying signature cocktail was a potent recipe for a relationship blackout! Like, we were having the best time, then *boom*!

A year later, if I would see him walking down the street, the man who left me breathless, that I wanted to marry, that I couldn't live without, is now just someone I used to know.

Inside of my relationships, there was always a push-and-pull dynamic. One minute I'm in, the next I'm out. It looked something like this: "I need you. No, no, I don't; I'm independent. I need you; no, actually, I'm fine. I need you; I tell you what, go fuck yourself."

When wounded in childhood, we become disconnected from ourselves. We cannot generate a sense of safety, containment, and adequate emotional stability from within to soothe and stabilise ourselves. This means we either start clinging or start running! Me, I was the Olympic style runner in the family.

Our past wounds around close relationships left us with an emotional deficit. This means you might experience yourself as lacking something inside. As if you are only half, not a whole person with access to a full set of emotional resources.

This means relationships can leave you anxious, insecure and afraid of being abandoned. You may not be conscious of this, but your relationships will soon reveal this to you. You will experience a lot of pain, heartache, repetitive negative patterns, toxicity, rejection, cruelty and unreciprocated love.

> There are only two types of people in this world. The ones who are traumatised and know it and the ones who are traumatised and don't know it.
>
> -Dr Gabor Mate

If events from your past left you disconnected from your inner power and emotional resources, you are likely seeking relationships for self-serving purposes. You seek relationships for emotional food and healing.

By emotional food and healing, I mean, you are looking for the self-worth, confidence, validation, acceptance, guidance, protection and safety you cannot generate from within to stabilise and settle you when you feel empty or hurt in your relationship.

Are you looking for someone to change your life? Make it easier? More exciting? Stabilise you? Whatever you might be looking for in your relationships, the truth is we have to learn to give ourselves what we are most seeking from others. Otherwise, we seek relationships for narcissistic supplies, not companionship and mutual caring.

Any successful relationship has to start with self-love, because when we have self-love we can implement proper boundaries. Boundaries help us to communicate our needs and non-negotiables. But you cannot ask a woman who is disconnected from herself to set boundaries because it is terrifying for her. She doesn't not fully have herself. If she lets go of him, she feels she has nothing.

Events of the past can prevent us from connecting with ourselves. When disconnected from ourselves, we are disconnected from or own gut responses. We are disconnected from our inner radar. We are looking outside of ourselves for answers. We are looking outside of ourselves for a sense of worthiness, belonging, and self-acceptance, value and confidence. We inevitably look to our partners to compensate for these felt inner deficits.

> Powerfully positive psychological change can be experienced as a result of struggling with highly challenging, highly stressful life experiences past or present.
>
> - Richard Tedeschi
>
> Founder of Post Traumatic Growth theory

Some women also subconsciously have children to stay busy and disconnected from themselves. From the pain they carry deep inside. The children continue filling them up emotionally. This way, they are guaranteed a distraction from self forever unless they choose to wake up and face themselves with help.

Hey, no judgment here. We all run from pain. We stop paying attention to how we feel and our lives. We avoid negative feelings like the plague and get hooked using a positive mindset to avoid our difficult feelings.

I mean, it's not surprising, is it? Who on earth chooses to feel emotional pain? Where do we learn how to experience our pain purposefully and intentionally - so we can use it to powerfully improve and expand our lives. So, many important questions. How do we use our pain to grow from?

Where do we learn how to give space to all our emotions, especially the unfelt dark ones that may have been ignored for far too long? Where do we learn how to love ourselves? How to fill ourselves emotionally? To soothe ourselves? That would be *nowhere!*

Who teaches us *how* to get proactive about our pain. How to *feel difficult emotions* and *how* to *process* them so we can grieve and be with them but not sit in them aimlessly only to become despondent and depressed?

Who educates us about the practical ways we can allow ourselves to feel our pain; tells that our pain has a fundamental link to our ability to grow and develop - pain puts us on a path towards deeper integration, to recover, acknowledge and assimilate the lost parts of ourselves, so we can function in a new, healthier ways in our relationships.

Emotional pain has a powerful purpose. We just need to know how to locate it and use it, to alchemise it into a deeper knowledge of self, greater power over self, and deeper wisdom on how to be *peacefully* and *acceptingly* with yourself.

We don't talk about the emotional pain we've incurred in childhood. We avoid discussing childhood woundings at family dinners, in schools, at the bar over cocktails. Culturally and socially, these conversations are left to the therapy room. No, but seriously, it's time to normalise talk about childhood trauma, interpersonal trauma, or attachment issues.

Our parents rarely sit us down and have the self-love talk either, not like they might have the birds-and-the-bees talk that helps us understand more about sex and boys. As if, somehow learning about sex and boys should take precedence over learning about self and relating to self lovingly.

Come to think of it; I was never given that talk, either. So this abstract concept of self-love seems to elude us all. Maybe that's why we avoid it because we don't know what the bloody hell it is. I mean really, what is self-love? What does it *actually* mean? And how do we *actually* do it?

Self-love and self-awareness are synonymous, for we cannot connect to something that we don't *know or understand.* To love ourselves then,

We had to learn how to bend without the world caving in

I had to learn what I got, and what I'm not and who I am.

- I Won't Give Up.

Jason Maraz

we must develop an inner ear; a *right* way to listen inwardly. Listen to ourselves and get to know how the ways we communicate with, and cater to, our inner needs, desires and promptings as they announce themselves. This is how we achieve true intimacy with ourselves. This is self-love.

We gradually learn to become more present to the currents within us, to let them flow without judgement. Our romantic relationships are our best teachers, for they generate the most tumultuous currents within. Disturbing the seabed of our emotions, bringing up old dormant wounds. Wounds that, if left unaddressed, will erode our self-esteem and disempower us.

Our romantic relationships tell us the precise climate and temperature of our internal world. For this reason, they are truly our blessings. By disturbing old wounds, they allow us to truly free ourselves from our past into a future without limits, where dreams can come true.

Over time we can learn to interpret the information our romantic relationships provide us with, to show us whatever we need to maintain peace and equilibrium within. Ladies, we have a vibrant emotional and spiritual eco-system within us. It is our job to keep it in pristine condition.

Psychotherapy tells us that self-love is something we should internalize from a loving parental environment. That if our primary carer was attuned and warm and loving, then we should automatically love ourselves, or have a high level of security and self-esteem.

I don't know about all of that. I think, to varying degrees, the only way we learn how to love ourselves is through the heartaches we suffer in our own adult relationships; and the flaws we come to know within ourselves. Our flaws teach us how to live with our imperfections and gradually learn to love all that we are. As long as we are growing, we are winning.

It is not so much about being in a bad relationship with someone else that counts. It is more about being in a *good* relationship with self. Because when we get into a healthy and empowered relationship with self, we inevitably find out what works for us.

For example, I never encourage clients to leave 'bad' relationships. It doesn't work. A woman will only walk away from a man mistreating her when she is ready and able to do so. I have worked with many women who stay until the end.

> *Take all the time you need to heal emotionally. Moving on doesn't take a day. It takes a lot of little steps to be able to break free from your broken self.*
>
> – Unknown

But even from this place of apparent powerlessness, these women carve out their own power in the relationship; certain spaces in their lived experience, which belong to them and must be honoured. Even if they do not have the relationship they want, even if part of them regrets choosing the man they are with, they find enough power to make it work until it no longer suits them.

Love will never be perfect. The choices we make in love, the ones that hurt, demonstrate something within us that needs time and gentle attention. We can learn from our relationship choices to love ourselves more deeply.

With every disappointment, every heartbreak, and every loss, we learn. We learn that we can endure; we learn the things we need to mend ourselves and feel better; we learn how to accept and be kind to ourselves, despite our flaws and defects of character; we learn that we are worthy of love even if we aren't perfect.

And we notice that the people, places and things in our lives, gradually change,to accommodate all the new things we are becoming, and all the new ways we are accepting ourselves. This is the process of self-love, a sacred process that takes time.

Become a woman who cares about having an unconditionally accepting and kind relationship with herself, a woman who cares about discovering what she needs most to assist her on her journey to becoming the best version of herself. What her mental patterns and triggers are, and how to evolve beyond the unhealthy and wounded parts of her that keep her stuck is the goal.

> **Tip:** Take some time away from dating or any intense relationship you might be having while you go through these twelve weeks. This is rehab. If you are serious about getting clean from leaning on the men in your life for energy, withdraw, and give yourself this short time. Perhaps for the first time ever.

Now, take a deep breath, channel Fergie, and repeat after me three times.

> *I need some shelter of my own protection, baby*
> *[To] Be with myself and center*
> *Clarity, peace, serenity*
> *I hope you know, I hope you know*
> *That this has nothing to do with you*
> *It's personal, myself and I*
> *We got some straightenin' out to do*
> *And I'm gonna miss you like a child misses their blanket*
> *But I've got to get a move on with my life*
> *It's time to be a big girl now*

Big Girls Don't CryFergie

The path of self-love must be walked alone. Take baby steps until you learn how to take care of the younger parts of you still holding on to old hurts. Develop and cultivate a mentoring relationship between that younger part and the strong adult you. Whenever you feel yourself collapsing into a wounded younger self, call upon the adult woman within you and have a tender and reassuring conversation with yourself. Say things like, "I love you. I will never leave you. You are worthy. You do not have to do anything to deserve love. Tell me, I will listen."

This goal of learning the steps toward self-love is so much more important than having a relationship with any man. You can never be happy with a man, or in any relationship, until you reach it.

We seek progress, not perfection. You have begun your journey by reading this book. There is no coincidence you are reading this. Slow down and take your romantic relationship recovery seriously. Don't abandon *you* anymore or give yourself up to him for adoption. Take good care of yourself. You are an adult now and are your own responsibility.

> "For life makes no mistake and always gives man that which man first gives himself."
>
> - Neville Goddard

Besides, it doesn't work when we get into relationships half-baked and looking for a *man oven* to finish the job. This here, ladies, in an inside job. It requires solitude to allow something new to emerge.

We all have rules we live by. One is, never go food shopping when you are hungry. Why? Because you pick up a load of rubbish. It's the same with men. Never look for a man when you're emotionally hungry. You'll just pick up some junk that is not good for you.

And please don't rush into a relationship until you prioritize this whole process of how to love you and effectively manage your life. If you do get into a relationship before you are available to yourself, you cannot be available to your partner. Why? Well, because you are already in a bad romance with yourself. Unconsciously, you yearn for a partner only to be the buffer that forms a barrier between you and your inability to fulfill and heal yourself. I know you've heard it all before, like Sunshine Anderson, but seriously, this needs to be your next project. Let's call it Project Self.

Now, in Project Self, you can forget your troubles. Come on, be happy. You can use your past failures with the men you loved, or thought you loved, as mirrors. And this is where we discover exactly who we are and how our past still influences our relationships today.

Author and self-love Guru, Louise Hay, puts it this way: "Everything in your life, every experience, every relationship is a mirror of the mental pattern that is going on inside of you."

For example, experiences like the ways you abandoned yourself and allowed your partners to disrespect you. You stayed in relationships with men already in relationships with other women. You settled for less, didn't say what you needed fearing being abandoned. You over gave. You tried so hard. So, hard. Ignoring your inner knowing.

It's okay. Don't worry about it. I've been there, too, often. We just wanted to be loved, but, sis, first, you have to love yourself. That means rehab. That means taking time out, not dating, no talking to men who aren't right. Taking time out for you. Perhaps for the first time, you are ready to give yourself the love you deserve and put yourself in the strongest position to find love? Of course, you are. That's why you're here.

And so, without self-love, we:

- Look for love outside.

- Put all your energy into trying to get him to love you rather than *know* you.

- Settle for less.

- Get into a relationship to fill your emptiness.

- Search for a more pleasant inner environment.

- Lose focus on your own dreams and purpose.

- Overeat/drink/shop/whatever to fill yourself up.

- Focus on making your outside beautiful/perfect.

Eventually, he will lose interest or leave because he feels something is amiss. It's as if you're having an affair, and in a way, you are. You're not present for the relationship; you're too busy avoiding the wounded and damaged relationship with yourself.

And so, you learn the hard way that you can be loved only at a foundational level by you. How come you can't find that person to love you right, you say to yourself to your friends.

> *"You have peace,"* the old woman said, *"when you make it with yourself."*
>
> *- Mitch Albom*

> *Tip:* Think back to a painful relationship. Revisit the scenes and how they played out. The shit you put up with, the lies, the manipulation, the indifference, the cruelty, the coldness.

Find the strength within to sit with the pain of loss and abandonment, rejection, and cruelty. These things can show up in our lives because we are already abandoning, rejecting, and being cruel to ourselves. Relationships are our mirrors. The men we date treat us exactly how we treat ourselves. And if they are good to us but are not available to us, it's because we are good to ourselves but are not fully available to ourselves.

We often give ourselves to another to take care of. To validate, to guide us. We look for someone to follow. But we must guide and validate ourselves. Until you can face your own self-abandonment and say to yourself, "I am sorry. I love you. I will be here for you, I will not abandon you ever again," you will always experience abandonment, unavailability, rejection, and insecurity in your relationships. We have to learn to be for ourselves what we seek in others.

Tip; Make a list of how you want your ideal partner to show you how he cares for you and how you want him to treat you. Start treating yourself like that today.

Sis, it's not him. It's you. You need to love you right. He will then come along and be the yummy bonus cherry on top. It's exhausting trying to get someone else to make you feel happy, beautiful, lovable, worthy, or to make your inner world bearable. You can only do this for yourself. You already have an inner guidance system that will show you how. But more about that in chapter 3.

Trust me, I looked for love and validation, guidance, a sense of self-worth and power from men, most of my life. Not having a clue how to give these things to myself. I did this for many, many years. I didn't seek relationships to enhance my life and enjoy companionship and love. I sought relationships for help, sustenance and healing. That's a big NO, NO.

I was always desperately seeking love. I was needy, jealous, and insecure, but I was also financially independent and intolerant. Today I know how to give and receive love effectively. I've studied myself and learned how to be a safe person all round. I mean, I'm still bit jealous, but hey, nobody is perfect.

But I wasn't always like that. When the problems came, and come they did, I stood face-to-face with my double bind. Desperate to be loved, but perhaps when it counted most, I couldn't show the man how much I needed him in my life. Not without getting tongue-tied, using sex, gifts or manipulation, or some version of vulnerability I had prepared earlier. I was petrified of love, to afraid to depend on him. My experience was that the people I truly lived either died or left. I wasn't about to go down that road again, we'll that was my unconscious narrative. Would have been nice if I'd been given a memo.

Too much inner turmoil and insecurity took over my ability to be vulnerable, authentic, and rooted in my self enough to show up as I felt inside. I was not sure if I was coming or going.

It looked something like this:

"It's fine. Honestly, I'm not even sure about all of this, anyway. We're so different. I've been hurt before, so maybe this is why I'm so weird—I mean, afraid. Err, but I like you a lot. But I feel so stupid, and it's just pathetic. Don't get me wrong, I'm an intelligent woman. Perhaps that's the problem. I'm too much; people always find me too much. Well, to be honest, that's their problem if they don't like me. I'm a bit crap at really having a deep relationship. Well, not crap; that's an exaggeration. But, especially since my separation, I've not been myself. Deep down, I'm fine being single. I probably need to be single for a while, anyway. Oh gosh, you must think I'm perfectly certifiable. Honestly, it's fine. Right, then. Another cocktail?

Tip: Don't do this on a date.

The addictions, the rejection, the chasing men, the games, the heartache, the confusion. Phew, it was a very painful and brutal road to travel. After a therapy session, I often wondered how I got myself into yet another fine mess, and why am I the one who never gets chosen but always left? I couldn't see that so many if my partners were trying to chose me. Or that I was the one doing the leaving, nor could I see all the toxicity I was bringing to my relationships.

My excuse? I came from a dysfunctional family and I lost my mum too young. What about you? What's your excuse?

It's not an excuse. Our childhood sets the tempo for every relationship to follow unless we intervene on the unconscious and mental processes that drive this powerful trajectory.

Don't discredit what happened to you when you were a child. It was a trauma. Trauma is anything that overwhelms you. It could be:

If you were left alone, scared, and afraid as a child with no adult support.

- If you were neglected in any way.
- If your authenticity made others uncomfortable, and so they shut you down.
- If no one paid enough attention to you to protect you from bad things.
- If your hurt feelings went unnoticed.
- If you lived with an alcoholic or abusive parent, or one with mental health issues.
- If you lived with narcissistic parent/s.
- Or anything similar.

If you have experienced the above, you have experienced childhood trauma, also called developmental trauma, because such events will mess with your ability to develop naturally into an adult with the capacity to relate healthily without insecurity and fear.

The trauma you experienced has set a neurological imprint in your brain. This imprint tells you what to expect from love and relationships, and controls how you attach yourself in your romantic relationships. But if you enter authentic transformative recovery, like with using the steps in this book, you will experience a breakthrough.

Typically, when the single woman considers her love interest, she may ask herself questions like, What will he look like? What job will he have? Will he want kids? Often, she has not given herself the time and investment she requires to know herself more deeply, become her best friend, and get in touch with the more profound questions.

> "Trauma shapes our lives. It shapes the way we live, the way we love, and the way we make sense of the world. It is at the root of our deepest wounds. Virtually all our afflictions, mental illnesses, physical diseases stem from trauma. Trauma distorts our view of reality and leaves us stuck in contraction, defense, and reactivity. It compromises our capacity to be in the moment, to be present to our relationships, and to fully take in the environment."
>
> - Dr. Gabor Mate

Tip: To deepen self-knowledge and learn what you need in love, ask yourself questions like these below. I've proved a few responses to get you thinking:

Q: How do I create an environment every day that supports me in becoming the most protective, tender, and generous partner to myself?

A: Start with journaling. Imagine some of your emotions are toxic and need to come out like vomit or diarrhoea - it needs to come out on the page. Release all your stuff into your journal. Do it every morning and night.

Q: How do I turn toward my inner environment for replenishment and healing when feeling unloved and alone?

A:Pray, watch something funny, take a walk, get silent. Silence and laughter are key. Just sit there. It might be uncomfortable at first, but soon the peace and replenishment comes.

Q: Has my past affected my ability to love myself and others?

A: Take a minute to think about your parents' relationship and /or relationship with siblings? Do you see the dynamics of your childhood repeating in your adult relationships. For example in issues around communication, trust, insecurity, self-worth?

Q: What specific obstacles make my romantic relationships hard?

A: Think about how you show up in relationships, is it your wounded child self? Are you jealous, controlling, passive, over giving, demanding, critical, avoidant, untrustworthy?

Q: Who must I forgive to release my reactive behaviours?

A: Is it your father? Mother? Ex? Siblings? Our ability to love without drama is inextricably linked to the level of forgiveness we have afforded to those we feel have hurt us. Unresolved childhood and adult issues are poison to our relationships.

Forgiveness is necessary if we wish to move forward and create happy healthy relationships. So, get ready to write a few letters to the people who have hurt you, dead or alive. Write to your parents telling them you forgive them and what you forgive them for. Tell them you are sorry for blaming the for so long as you understand they did their best. Seal it and burn it. It is a letting go ceremony.

> "Knowing yourself is the beginning of all wisdom."
>
> - Aristotle

Then write to your significant, Ex. Write what I call a responsibility letter. Get real honest. Explain the areas where you betrayed yourself and ignored your inner knowing while in the relationship with them. Explain where you made yourself a victim and gave him all the power. You can send these or not. It's up to you.

Q: What lies beneath my triggers?

A: Look out for the next time something happens that makes you very reactive and feel taken over by a powerful emotion like; Anger, sadness, hurt, aggressive or any powerful emotion. Trace this back to a relationship or incident where the dynamics were similar. Can you locate the rot of your trigger?

I want you to pull focus. Take the attention off the man and put it back on you. Have you ever noticed how the questions you might typically have about your next relationship are concerned with your *prospective partner's* suitability rather than your suitability for intimacy and relationship?

I often hear women say, "I just haven't found the right person yet" when responding to questions about their single status. But do we ever ask ourselves if we are the right person for love?

> *Tip:* Write down two character flaws that your ex-partner would point out about you. What did he say you do? Maybe he said, you never listen to him, or you don't communicate, whatever it was, see if you can link that behaviour back to a childhood relationship or dynamic, or make a thread between that behaviour/s and your childhood. Add it to our Facebook community when you're done.

Everything depends on how you feel about yourself.

PART 1

Have you ever noticed how not until you experience a deep heartbreak do you seem to connect more deeply with yourself and think more deeply about the answers to the questions above?

It is usually after a heartbreak, or when a relationship is hurting, that you vow never to give your power away to any man again. Inevitably you do because you were not thorough enough with your self-investigation and didn't give yourself enough "single" time before letting another lover into your heart.

Can you slow down and stay single long enough to tend to the wounds that keep causing you to feel insecure and powerless in your relationships?

Ultimately your loneliness triggers a desire to separate from yourself and give yourself to another to take care of. This self-abandonment takes precedence over your need to sit with your pain, hurt, and damage, and accept yourself. By simply allowing yourself to resist leaping from yourself, but instead releasing some of your hurt, you build a foundation of wholeness.

So, many women I talk to tell me their world feels empty, bored, stagnant, and lacks excitement. They await a partner to provide this. Never wait for a man to light up your world—set it on fire yourself.

Fill up your life with excitement and adventure. If you are bored and have a life that lacks excitement, it's because you haven't figured out how to tap into your purpose or move out of fear to pursue the things you want.

> A busy, vibrant, goal-oriented woman is so much more attractive than a woman who waits around for a man to validate her existence.
>
> - Mandy Hale

Getting into a relationship will not remove any of these issues, it will only put them on temporary pause. Soon they will resurface again, but this time within the relationship, you might feel depressed or anxious because the old discontentment you feel has not gone away.

The loneliness, the low self-esteem, the lack of purpose and direction all come back. Nobody can save you from yourself except for you.

Do not step into yet another mistaken union, where more heartbreak awaits. It is time to take responsibility for how you are showing up in love and stop hurting yourself.

No matter our background, the loss of power a woman experiences in her relationships with men does not discriminate. Reclaiming your power and self-love as a single woman is not about having control over men but is about having power over yourself and making sure your first attention is on you.

> The relationship you have with you is the most precious one that you will ever have. And the best way to love yourself is to grow a kind, loving, and mentoring connection between your strong, wise adult self and those tender, younger parts of you that may still be holding hurts and fears about your goodness, your power, and your worthiness to be loved.
>
> - Katherine Woodward Thomas

So, when he shows up, no matter how damn fine he is, or how many boxes he ticks, you stay effortlessly rooted in your values and priorities. Any man serious about you will wait and honour your terms. If he walks, don't worry about it; he's not for you.

If you feel worthy and valuable and unique and deserving of receiving the best, you will draw the man of your dreams to you without even trying. Why? Because you are full, able to nourish and soothe yourself. You are your own best friend and have become your own soul mate.

You stay busy and vibrant. You pray for love, wish for love, but you don't sit around waiting for it. Get out there and live. Get out of your head and into your life. The minute you make this shift, a king of a man will appear the minute the queen in you emerges from within.

This is why, for many of us, men are so fundamental on the journey of self-love. They are our mirrors, reflecting the self-love we lack within. Unconsciously we attract partners who will pull on our strings and draw out the root of our issue. Freud believed this was a compulsion to resolve the original problem. But more about that later.

Through the men we have loved and their resistance to play our little game, we get to experience our self-betrayal, our consistent abandonment of self, our tendency to wallow in self-pity, our desperation, denial, self-neglect, and powerlessness. We then get to love ourselves and restore ourselves to wholeness and watch with awe and excitement as the sexy brother of our dreams saunters into our lives without trying. Damn, this is good. I will buy my own book.

Now take a deep breath, channel Ariana Grande, and repeat after me three times:

> One taught me love
> One taught me patience

And one taught me pain
Now I'm so amazing
Say I've loved and I've lost
But that's not what I see
So, look what I got
Look what you taught me
And for that I say

Thank u, next
Thank u, next
Thank u, next
I'm so fucking grateful for my ex

So, seriously, thanks to your awful and naughty little exes, your issues have been revealed to you. You have the opportunity now to restore yourself to wholeness. Think about Amy Winehouse, whose rehab song encouraged me to write this book. Like many of us, she fell head over heels in love and lost herself in the process.

Perhaps the same applies to Caroline Flack. These beautiful girls poured their lack of self-love onto their relationships like gasoline on a fire. If they had been still and honest, they could have transformed their lives for the better, but they didn't get to spin this thing around. But you do. Being single is a blessing; it is the opportunity to take time out and examine yourself more deeply.

Amy Winehouse and Caroline Flack are extreme cases, let their lives not be in vain. You may feel your situation is a million miles away from theirs. But we have all lost ourselves in love, and at times our pain was unbearable. In AA, they often say to look for the similarities and not the differences.

May the life of these leading lights teach all single women everywhere to put themselves first. To admit when they see a problem behaviour within themselves in the way they are loving. These beautiful, talented girls had everything— money, looks, talent, personality. Everything except the ability to admit there was a problem and seek help to repair and heal.

> "You're not responsible for the poor parenting you may have received as a child.
>
> Yet...
>
> You are responsible for how you're keeping alive that legacy in your relationships, and how you choose to treat yourself today."
>
> - Katherine Woodward Thomas
>
> Katherine Woodward Thomas

So, you've taken step one. Admitted there is problem, and that problem is with self-love. Well done. It is a necessary concession before transformation can happen. You are getting closer to *you* with each word you read.

Accepting you have a problem is the first step on the ladder of self-love because legit, loving yourself is crazy, sexy cool, and it is the biggest, baddest secret to bagging the man of your dreams.

Your twelve-step journey must start with honesty, with an admission that your best thinking in love got you nowhere. From Amy Winehouse's tragic story, we understand that letting go of the men we think we love is difficult. But let go we must for our health and mental and emotional well-being.

Men do not have the power to heal your childhood wounds or meet the needs you present to them in your relationships. To some degree, a good man can help with healing. But ultimately, the work must be done by you. By reading this book and doing the exercises, you are choosing you. You are *actually* loving yourself in practice.

No one is responsible for us once we are adults. We have to accept ourselves, love ourselves, and protect ourselves from the forces that threaten to destabilize our commitment to loving ourselves unconditionally.

How on God's green earth did I get here?

As children, we consistently take in love of our mother or primary carer, or at least we should. We take in this love as one would a glass of water, drinking and drinking it daily. Spitting it out at times, but always knowing it is there for our consumption. Over time, we continue to internalize *taking in* our mother's love. We become reassured that we are loved and worthy of another's time and attention.

This *knowing* becomes part of our makeup. The love we receive becomes a part of who we are. We are filled with love that takes on its own life within us, fortifying us with power and strength to mitigate the good and bad in our relationships.

As we develop into young adulthood, the symbiotic process that started as our mother's love and reverie become our own self-love and self-esteem, forming the very core of our relational identity.

> *They fuck you up, your mum and dad. They may not mean to, but they do.*
>
> *They fill you with the faults they had and add some extra, just for you.*
>
> *- Philip Larkin*

You can see how this core could be critical in our relationships; it is this love we depend upon for our ability to move through life's difficult times without becoming destabilized. The more of this love you drank in as a child, the more secure and balanced you are in your adult relationships.

This inner love helps us to take care of ourselves, forgive ourselves, honor and protect ourselves, and ensures that the people we allow into our lives do the same. It also helps us to be safe people to be in relationship with.

Unfortunately, we're not all so lucky. Many of us come from homes where relationships were not so healthy, to varying degrees. We were taught how to relate to ourselves by people who may have struggled with loving themselves and making healthy choices.

In an environment where parents did not have good enough relational skill, you might have unwittingly picked up messages from your parents about the world and your value or worth. Messages such as people are bad or untrustworthy or that we are not lovable or worthy of another's time, attention, and care.

This I'm-not-lovable software runs throughout our lives, which means we develop highly attuned antennae to pick up the frequency of men who will help us re-experience the feelings that mirror our childhood experience—men who communicate the same messages to us we received in our childhood, whether consciously or unconsciously. Although painful, this is familiar and can make us feel safe.

When we feel disappointment, rejection, abandonment, inadequacy, shame, and unworthiness with the men we love, on some level we will feel at home if we experienced these things in our childhood home.

The more we feel these negative emotions, the more we cling to these men for validation and love, as if trying to rewrite our history.

Change is impossible without education and implementing steps like those in this book, therapy, or some other recovery and healing process. We don't possess an inner power (or enough self-love) to mitigate the good and the bad adequately. Instead, we get carried away with these unconscious forces like a feather on the wind.

Let me share my first relationship story with you. I hope you will see how powerlessness, codependency, and self-abandonment happens to us all. I made many mistakes in the name of love. It hurts, and it's shameful. It brings tears to my eyes that my daughter will read this stuff about her mummy one day. But if I can teach her anything, it is to live authentically and bravely. To know that the people she attracts are merely mirrors of what's happening inside her. But God willing, I'll be there to guide and watch over her, unlike with my mother and me.

Powerlessness

Meet Renaldo Luigi

The first man I thought I loved - Until we love ourselves, it is not love - it is codependency

Location: Rome, Italy

Hotness: 10/10

Humiliation factor: 7/10

Pain factor: 10/10

I met Renaldo at Cafe Du Paris in 2018. It was a very exclusive nightclub in London. It was the place to be with my best friend, Zara from university. We were two spoiled girls on a mission to have fun and fall in love. He was one of a group of impeccably dressed playboy Italians. They reeked wealth with their Montecristo Cigars. Rolexes, and crisp, white tailored shirts. They were bold, elegant, and beautiful.

Renaldo was supremely confident. He wasted no time asking me to dance. I accepted, flattered by the way he protectively guided me to the dance floor as though I belonged to him. I like that kind of thing.

The more obstacles you face and overcome, the more times you falter and get back on track, the more difficulties you struggle with and conquer, the more resiliency you will naturally develop. There is nothing that can hold you back, if you are resilient.

As we danced, I peered around excitedly to see if I could see my friend Anya. He cupped his hand and gently guided my chin back to his face, so we were eye to eye and said in his jealous, solid Roman accent, "Look at me while we dance." I was, like, *Whoa, intense!*

Besides his striking good looks (six-three, and he looked like Richard Gere) and sizzling sexiness, the second thing that struck me about Fabio and this group was that they were smoking something that smelled very peculiar. I discovered later that it was cocaine. I'd never touched a class A drug in my life. Not until I met Fabio, that is. You see where this is going.

Renaldo invited me to join him at his house in Italy. I'll never forget him writing his number on a Cafe de Paris white velvety coaster. The following day my friend called me and screamed into my very hungover ear, "Babe! You know we've always wanted to go to Italy! Here's our chance. Let's do it!" I was, like, "Hmmm. Okay."

I was managing my Dad's nightclub while he was in Jamaica (another story). My mum had died a few years earlier, and I was solo. I wasn't the type to go stay in some stranger's house, so I grabbed a few thousand pounds from the safe in my dad's office (another story again). Zara grabbed her dad's credit card, and buono, in time we'd booked a swanky hotel in Rome, jumped on a plane, and off we went. Living *la vida loca*!

Connecting the dots between Childhood, Fantasy, and the Men you choose

When we got to Italy, Renaldo came to see us immediately. He was just as handsome as I'd remembered. But his English was not good at all. Conveniently, I didn't remember that bit. With hindsight, it is interesting that I remembered his good looks but not that his English was terrible. And I ignored that I spoke no Italian. Yet none of this deterred me from embarking on a *relationship* with this man.

In a very concrete way, I was setting myself up to repeat a situation from my childhood, where this man and I would have no way to address anything of real substance because we didn't speak the same language! In my childhood, I never witnessed intimacy between my parents. I saw two people who spoke two very different languages, even though they were both speaking English. Here I was, choosing a man, embarking on a romantic relationship with no prospect of ever having any real intimacy. Any real communication. This is me recreating a childhood dynamic.

The problem is, we don't always remember the ins and outs of our childhood. We don't know unless we have therapy how to make these critical connections between what happened then and how we are *making* it happen again now, as if under spell.

> *Love is every bit as violent and dangerous as murder.*
>
> *- Knut Hamsun*

What we are doing in these twelve weeks involves an effort to break this cycle of repetition by helping you remember where it all started. Helping you go back to your childhood and the dynamics you were enmeshed in because you are repeatedly recreating these dynamics in your relationships.

This is what happened to me; I am describing my account of the relationships between Renaldo and me. Even though lasting love is what I wanted so desperately, it seemed I had no conscious power to focus my intention and create the environment for a committed, loving, communicative relationship.

Instead, I abandoned myself and my needs and priorities. I dropped my heart and my future into the hands of this stranger to draw up the terms of engagement, the direction, and all aspects of our relationship. I left it up to him to do what he wanted to do with me! Utter powerlessness. But I wasn't in it for power. I was in it to re-experience abandonment, longing, disappointment, and loss. Those were the dynamics of my childhood, which I wanted. Unconsciously, of course. Sounds sadistic, right?

Fast-forward a few days, and we're on a boat to his parents' *other* place in Sardinia. This man opened my eyes to Italy in a way I'd never experienced any country with a lover, and I've had a few long-distance relationships in my time. It was romantic and beautiful, and I remember he would always play music from his favorite singer, Luca Carboni, as we'd drive around the city in his BMW.

One night I was chattering away, as usual, unable to just be still with him or myself, and he peered at me, searching, almost as if he was trying to see the real me. He said in his thick accent, "Nancy, don't speak. Take in the city." Embarrassed by my apparent need to nervously fill the silence, I just stopped talking and breathed.

I allowed myself to connect the world around me for a moment. But checking in with myself, being still and connected was not something I did often back then, especially in the moment with a man I like. Mostly, I was not present in those situations, just a shell of me was.

So, we continued our adventure. We visited unique restaurants in Costa Smeralda and Porto Cervo and enjoyed the black truffle, the sweetest tomatoes I had ever tasted, delicious fish, mouth watering pasta dishes served with tender and seasoned meat - even the bread was outstanding.

It was sublime. We had a blast and lots and lots of sex, but little talking. Still, I felt I powerfully connected with this man. There was a strong connection; it was lust and that was all it was. So, often we mistake passion for love.

One night we went to his friend's villa in Sardinia. I think he said something about his friend's father being a manager in Formula 1 racing. I remember little about the night except when he brought out a glass dish with lines of cocaine on it. I had seen coke before—please, I'm a Londoner, plus my first job out of university was for a record label, where they did it all the time. I'd never been interested in the drug, and I've always been too afraid to try.

This time, it was different. It was glamorous. We were in a beautiful villa in Sardinia, a warm Mediterranean breeze blew through the vast open spaces. I felt beautiful and safe, but I wasn't safe. It was a fantasy. Fantasy is that delicious icing on a cake that looks impeccable but will lead you to a slow poisonous death if you don't wake up out of its spell.

I was in danger, making bad decisions that could threaten my life and health. I fell in lust and intrigue with a man who did not know or love me. Fantasy in love is more potent than any drug. I created my reality; I lived in a false world where everything was okay and

Intensity-seeking is an enslavement of our own perpetuation. When we step out of the delirium of always seeking someone new and meet the same old sad and lonely child within, our healing journey begins.

Exhausting ourselves with novelty is a defense against our deepest pain, one that we cannot outrun. But once we stop and feel our losses, we can begin our healing journey and be the authentic, joyous person we were born to be.

- Alexandra Katehakis

honest and correct. The total opposite of what was going on. When I think back to that poor motherless child, it hurts. So, vulnerable in her search for love. But, I also high-five her.

Writing this book is making a bold declaration of reclaiming my power and reclaiming hers. By writing this book and telling this relationship story, I've gone back to that younger girl, and I have given myself a voice. I have also gone back with her in my arms, a strong, protective and competent mother. The younger wounded parts of me are in the best hands today. I take care of me, I do not loan myself out looking for foundational safety, stability and love from anyone. Not anymore.

My inner little girl is mine, her emotional hunger, insecurity, fear, and low self-esteem. Those characteristics all belong to me. I have deep intimacy with myself, and as if I e travelled backwards in time to rescue that girl in Italy, to tell my story on my terms. I am sorry for her pain and that she was all alone without me to mentor, guide and love her.

Today, I am on a lifelong journey to wholeness almost twenty years later. No need to keep seeking new relationships to perpetuate my childhood trauma. No more drama. I vow I will never abandon myself again. It has taken me a long, long time to get here, with many broken promises to myself and many bumps along the way. I imagine there will be more. Is this a good time to revisit the little girl in you, to go back and claim her and give her a voice?

Renaldo was the first serious case of codependency and self-abandonment that I remember. There were many more to come. I continued to fall in love and get entangled in relationships rejecting and painful. Either I was doing the damage, or he was.

With Renaldo, I ignored all the signs. Whenever that still, small voice within whispered its caution, I would simply apply another thick layer of fantasy to keep it quiet. Here I was with my best friend. I was also with a man I considered my Prince Charming. But there was no actual evidence this man cared about me and wanted to protect me; it was all in my head.

I was falling into a dark and dangerous place—the cocaine, the alcohol, in a foreign country, no family to hold me accountable. Yet I was tricking myself into believing this whole scene in this exquisite place was fairy tale, a place full of love, truth, and safety. I had that line up my nose before you could say Leonardo DiCaprio.

Cut to me at his house in Rome. He would go to work all day, and I'd just sit there at his home. I remember waking up, going to get breakfast, and finding nothing much in the fridge. I felt hurt he had made no effort, even though he knew I was coming from London. But the hurt didn't last; I pushed it away. More icing.

I put a few things together from the fridge, but it was hardly adequate. It wasn't the first time. It never occurred to me to confront him about not providing for me or insist that I fly out to see him only when he took time off work. I mean, it was his dad's company. I'm sure he could have managed time away.

As a child, I couldn't identify my needs. I guess on some level I thought it was his job to take care of me and identify my needs. If he didn't provide for me, I guess a part of me thought it must be ok. If *he* thinks it's okay.

I abandoned my being and put it in another's hands to take care of. Maybe it was too difficult to stay with me. I had never seen a woman in my family show up powerfully for herself with men. I had no model to emulate. Perhaps I was too hurt or too damaged by the volatile relationship of my parents, the infidelity of my father, the abandonment from both parents on some level, losing my mother at seventeen. Maybe it was too hard to say, *Nancy, I love and accept you. I will never leave you. I will re-raise you. I've got you.* But I did not have this language at my disposal.

I didn't say much about Fabio's inconsiderate behaviour, but deep down, being mistreated or not considered hurt. I couldn't seem to articulate it to him, or even think about it in my head without making excuses for him.

I just didn't value myself enough to ask for what I wanted. Maybe I was afraid I would lose him. Or maybe I should have told him I had spent time and money to fly to Rome to be with him and that he should spend more time with me or take care of me and my needs. When it was the other way around, I went out of my way for him.

When a woman lacks self-love, there is plenty of room for predatory and narcissistic men to sneak into their heart. Without self-love, without self-knowledge and education, without therapy, self-delusion and mistreatment by others will happen, especially betrayal of yourself.

Many women move into fantasy or delusion to compensate for the lack of self-love within. It's not a conscious decision. It's like a default setting. A woman is perpetually looking outward for love, sincerely wanting genuine love, but is driven to attach herself to a man whose behaviour will conform to the dysfunctional pattern she experienced in her past.

It's a wicked double bind—kind of the one I described at the beginning of this chapter. So, in place of possessing inner self-love, the default is to seek the first and most crucial attachment dynamic she ever knew. A painful relationship. Because while it is dysfunctional, it is home to her. The first heartbreak she ever had; it's familiar and familial. Without the right help, she will struggle to modify this repetitive cycle.

Attachment theory teaches us that infants have a biological drive to seek proximity to a protective adult. When that adult is not so protective but is instead abandoning or cruel. The child will still seek proximity to the mother while learning to normalise the neglect of her feelings and the adults rejecting behaviour.

The child adapts itself to the adult dysfunctional behaviour by disappearing her own needs. This cutting off one's own needs in childhood is a way of meeting the critical need a child has for closeness. This is where the roots of codependency and maladaptive adaptation form.

We've all seen the mother puffing away on a cigarette and screaming and swearing at her child to shut up. Still, the child determinedly pursues the mother, face red, eyes streaming tears, arms outstretched. The child is distressed, crying, and repeating robot-like, "Mummy, Mummy, Mummy, please hug me."

At times like these, the child undergoes an internal shift. Her own emotional pain is no longer critical now; the priority has become getting some physical closeness to her mummy. The child has to ignore its own need for empathy or warmth, to fulfil her need for proximity to her mother. Abandoning one's feelings in pursuit of love. See where it all starts?

If you experienced confusing, frightening, or inconsistent emotional communication during infancy, or, if your caregiver was unable to consistently comfort you or respond to your needs, you're more likely to have experienced an unsuccessful or insecure attachment. Infants with insecure attachment often grow into adults who have difficulty understanding their own emotions and the feelings of others, limiting their ability to build or maintain stable relationships. They may find it difficult to connect to others, shy away from intimacy, or be too clingy, fearful, or anxious in a relationship.

- Helpguide International

It's like this, "I'll put up with your neglect, cruelty, and pain, as long as you don't leave." We take these mental processes with us into adulthood.

Remember this powerful anthem, "Just Be Good to Me" by The S.O.S. Band.

> *You may have many others*
> *But know when you're with me, you are all mine*
> *Friends seem to always listen*
> *To the bad things that you do*
> *You never do them to me Ohh*
> *People always talking about, reputation.*
> *I don't care about your other girls*
> *Just be good to me.*

SOS Band

My understanding of this song is this girl is in fantasy. She is making excuses for a man she is in love with so she doesn't have to face reality, which I imagine she doesn't have the power to face. She doesn't have the power to walk away because she feels her life would be unbearable without him.

Fantasy is an adaptation we make to stay close to the person we have become attached to. Fantasy distorts our reality and our ability to have a mature and meaningful life. It's a kind of insanity. We'll get more deeply into that in week 2.

Back to Renaldo. Several of us went to a restaurant one night, and we were seated, glancing over our menus. I felt beautiful and confident. I then noticed him light up like a Christmas tree. His eyes were bright and wide, and a warm smile was spreading across his face. He seemed to smile at someone in the distance, who he immediately beckoned over to our table.

> "The most confused you will ever get is when you try to convince your heart and spirit of something your mind knows is a lie."
>
> - Shannon L. Alder

I squinted my eyes to see who he was waving at, and as she came into focus. I could immediately feel myself shrinking inside. She was a tall, slim brunette strolling over to our table as if she were in a slow-motion scene from a Chanel catwalk. Her dress sense was elegant, with her chic, beige silk blouse with just the right buttons undone, black leather pencil skirt, black patent high-heel shoes.

I felt like a little girl in her presence. As I watched her shake my hand and smile warmly at me, then continue talking to Fabio, so calm and relaxed and at ease in her skin, I knew she had something I didn't. This was obvious to all of us at the table. Plus, that I couldn't speak Italian or understand a word they were saying was infantilizing.

I knew I would have what she had one day, and the only problem was I had no idea what it was or how to get it. Now I know it was self-love. It's impossible to mistake a woman who loves herself; she possesses an unmistakable energy and presence. She oozes confidence, self-esteem, and inner joy that makes her beauty beam from the inside out. Today I have that, but I got it a long time after Renaldo. That's why I wrote this book, not just for my own closure, but also to spare you that time and pain.

I never felt quite adequate with Renaldo. One night after a few lines of soft coke, we went to a beautiful club in Mayfair London. Cocaine always caused me anxiety, so I felt unwell. I had clocked the connection between Fabio and the hostess for our table; just the way they were exchanging glances, it was clear what was going on. I felt shaky, so I told him I needed to go; he was livid and stormed out of there. We had a huge argument, but it made no real difference. Another time we were shopping at a mall, and he kept walking in front of me, like I was some puppy dog who should walk behind him.

There were many of these episodes where I wasn't loved, cherished, or respected by him. Do you see the pattern here? I wasn't loved, cherished, or respected by me.

It seemed I was always waiting for him to call me, or I was calling him. I got on with my workday, but he was the most significant source of energy and excitement. He trumped everything else. I just couldn't match the aliveness I felt with him. My ambitions, projects, girlfriends, and everything moved firmly into second place.

It was as if he was my purpose. Having his love, winning his love, being attractive and sexy for him, being in his presence, trying to get his love. That's where my focus was. And that was in all my relationships prior and subsequent. Unless I was with a man who was fully available to me, then I had so much power and confidence, but not such a strong attraction. But that's another chapter.

My feelings for Fabio were more significant than anything else in my life, including my well-being and happiness. He said, "You're like a Ferrari with the wrong gas." I didn't take offence to the car analogy; I did not quite get it then, but I get it now. As time passed, I felt increasingly needy and wanted more. I was also developing another bad habit: cocaine.

> Rock bottom was the solid foundation on which I built my life.
>
> - J. K. Rowling.

For me, though, coke was just a bit of fun, more icing. I told myself I was in love, and I was fine. I wasn't doing it every day, only weekends, and not every weekend, just Friday nights in some club loo, thinking it was cute and rebellious. My drug issue wasn't Fabio's fault, and it was just a symptom of a deeper problem within me I could act out through the coke. I lacked self-love and needed something to fill it. An addiction is an attempt to feel peace, connection, and relieve suffering.

I had so much I wanted to escape from. My mother had died a few years before, and my father was favouring me over my sisters. My chronic and dangerous lack of self-love meant I did not have the resources to deal with the problems in my family, the emotional deprivation, the loss, powerlessness, the resentment. All these things demand we love ourselves to pull us through.

Self-love gives us the power to deal with these issues without internalising them and carrying them into our adult relationship as trauma. Without self-love, we become overly identified with the traumatised child, and she takes the driver's seat in our adult relationships. Self-love combined with a relationship with your higher power (more in chapter 2) is the remedy for this.

Fast-forward, we had planned to spend New Year's Eve together, and at the time, I was living in an apartment on top of my dad's nightclub while he was flat shopping for me. I rented an expensive serviced apartment for Fabio and me to see the new year in. It had been a year that we'd been together. I'd met his family, and he'd met mine. In my fantasy, things were going well. But neither of us communicated beyond sending each other love songs and "I miss you. I love you. When can you come and visit?"

A few days before his arrival, I called him to finalise his visit. The woman I was renting the apartment from was pressuring me to sign the contract. I called him to tell him he needed to confirm that he was coming, or we'd lose the apartment (that I was paying for!). I remember his phone ringing and no answer.

It was very unusual for Renaldo not to answer, and if he didn't respond immediately, he always called back quickly. But this time, I just couldn't get through to him. I tried again and again, no answer. I was confused. That night was the longest ever, and I called and called and called. Nothing.

The next day, nothing, and the next and the next. He'd just disappeared. After about 5 days, I was inconsolable. I had an instinct it was over, but my predominant feeling was that something must have happened to him. I called his friend in utter desperation. I was confident he was dead. I mean, otherwise, why wouldn't he call me? I moved from feeling he was no longer alive or in the hospital to racking my brain, trying to remember our last conversation and whether I might have said or done something wrong. I kept asking myself, *Why is this happening?*

As his friend's phone rang in that familiar Italian ring tone, I held my breath. Finally, his friend answered. My desperation was palpable, my voice breathy. "Paulo, have you heard from Fabio?" Pause.

Paulo responded in a cheerful and blasé voice, "Ah, *ciao*, Nancy. Sure, I spoke with Renaldo yesterday." I was crushed. My heart dropped into my feet like a ton of bricks. I became all at once dizzy and nauseous.

Over time, I lost about two stone and ramped up my cocaine and alcohol use. I cried for a whole year. Soon, I ended up in a twelve-step program.

Five years later, Renaldo got in contact. He told me he couldn't have continued the way things were, that the language barrier made him feel like a child. Interestingly, he took the steps he needed to when the relationship felt like it wasn't serving him—something I could not do.

He flew over and stayed with me for a week around New Year's Eve at my place in Notting Hill. We had a great time. I was stronger and more assured. After our time together, he disappeared again. I wasn't too hurt. It made me laugh. As we get healthier, things get clearer. We are more resilient and more able to see other people's stuff as exactly that - their stuff! We see that the things others do to us have little to do with us and everything to do with their dysfunction, fear, and cowardice.

Childhood heartbreak

Have you wondered what happens to your mind when you get caught up in fantasy? Like, literally, where does your mind go? We tell ourselves we know what we're doing, as if we know something everyone else doesn't. Our friends can see it; anyone who knows about the relationship sees it but us. It's not that bad, and I don't have a problem; I'm in control. I get it now; I'll never do that again.

Can you hear that Amy Winehouse song? "I ain't got the time, and if my daddy thinks I'm fine." Oh, ladies, we must stop making excuses. We are hurting ourselves by staying with these men that do not reciprocate our love. We should never beg for love or ask to be loved or cared for. You are worthy of love. Period.

Fabio knew there was something wrong with me on an emotional level. He sensed my lack of self-love from very early on. Men are good at that. This is why he said I was like a Ferrari without the right fuel. That's what many of us girls are like, the most magnificent creations running on low self-esteem and therefore performing at a meager standard in our lives!

It's time to power up with self-love. That's the gas you need. It will allow you to function optimally and have a life filled with joy, abundance, peace, true love and a whole lot of va, va, Voom!

It took me a long time to realize I had a problem. I wasn't resisting the truth. I was so blind to these facts about myself. I didn't know I was unconsciously bound to a childhood consciousness that believed I was not worthy of love, a consciousness that believed love had to be difficult in many ways.

> "One can choose to go back toward safety or forward toward growth. Growth must be chosen again and again; fear must be overcome again and again."
>
> - Abraham Maslow

I genuinely thought the problem was with the men I was dating and would be different next time. I was so keen to change my world. I didn't know then that if I wanted my world to change, I t would be enchant on me to change myself first.

We may have made bad choices. We may have given ourselves away for free without getting much or nothing in return. But we are not deterred. Because there is nothing on this planet as powerful and beautiful as love. We, the girls who love too much, are the smart ones. We know a good thing when we see it. We just need to get the right pieces and put them together. We are hopeless romantics, and, yes, we still want love after all the heartache and loss. You bet on your nelly, we bloody do. We will never give up on love.

The formidable Nelson Mandela teaches us that "Love comes more naturally to the human heart than the opposite." Love is everything, but it's also compelling and dangerous and destructive when it's turned upside down by a wounded soul. So, we have got to get right with ourselves first. Baby steps, remember?

And when we've learned to love ourselves and ensure that our first attention is always on us, we can get out there and unleash all the passion we have inside because women like us are filled to the brim with passion, and obsession and servitude, and submission and dry throatiness, and the heart beating that love brings. We are the epitome of the feminine goddess, ready and willing to receive by our hunter man. To be taken and owned. To be protected and loved.

Yet we shall not forget our tendency to self-abandon. We shall remain stable, and when destabilized, we shall move into solitude and prayer to soothe and recover ourselves, emerging stronger and stabilized. Ready to re-engage; ready to join our partner in an interdependent relationship, instead of a codependent, self-abandoning one. I salute you, my sisters. Never give up on love. Love may have hurt you initially, but you just see going full circle, and it will heal you in the end.

Tip: Single is the best damn thing that ever happened to you,

- Have fun as you fall in love with yourself.

- Feel beautiful, eat well, drink lots of water.

- Connect to your own arousal about yourself and your life.

- Feel the excitement of connecting to yourself.

- Exercise, pray, dress up in the house when you're by yourself. Dance, sing.

- Before you can get him to put a ring on it, you have got a put a ring on your own finger.

- Fall deeply in love with you.

- Learn to be for yourself what you seek in others.

- Write down ten reasons you want to spend the rest of your life with you.

The single woman myth

The single woman is not busying herself having sex with everyone's husband or any wanton stranger that tips his in her direction. Neither is she a sad and lonely, pathetic creature, with her living room curtain pulled back, gazing wearily through her window, waiting for a man to validate her life. These mythical creatures were concocted by a society deeply embedded in patriarchal structures and ideologies about women's worth, abilities, and place of belonging.

We single women reject that shit right out of the bag. We say fuck that. We are earnest in finding out what works for us in love; earnest in doing the inner healing work and taking our time to be ready for the king of a man we will attract once said work has launched.

We are not prepared to adhere to some patriarchal manifesto laying out the time, posture, age and way we should attach ourselves to a man.

When the single woman drafts her own manifesto, she realises that bringing structure into her life and doing the inner work around healing her relationship with men, money and self-love is the sexiest thing ever. The exact things that turn on a highly feminine woman are wshe has been shamed for wanting.

She wants a masculine man to own her, protect her, love her, and take control of some aspects of her. She wants to be a powerful, loving, attentive, patient, present mother. She wants more money, more love, more sex, and passion.

Single |sin•gle| (adjective) - Too fabulous to settle.

- Mandy Hale

More beauty and sexual prowess. The highly feminine woman can deepen self-love and intimacy with herself.

When she can align with the things that really turn her on. Ignoring all the shaming and rebuke that society slathers all over her for this appetite, she feels free.

The single woman is fiercely independent. She is a warrior who is not afraid to remain outside of the expected behavioural norms. She lifts her head, swings her hips, and walks with such grace and purpose, whether in pain or ecstasy. She is a true queen.

Bottom line, she is too fabulous to settle. Simple and true. Despite her desire for love, her passion, her femininity and softness, the single woman is a highly independent creature. She does not settle easily, which is why she is single. I find it increasingly frustrating to deal with the perceptions and stereotypes surrounding single women and who we are. Equally frustrating are the constraints that are attempted to be placed around the single

woman, her desires and appetite for life and love.

Perhaps society fears the single woman. She has not conformed. Sure, she wants love; she wants it badly. But ultimately, she would rather be alone than submit to the discomfort that a bad romance offers. She is unconsciously driven to relationships that allow her to have it all. And have it all she shall. If she does the inner work and healing required.

She is resilient and will not conform. Therefore, she is often the subject of pity, or the disingenuous, envious and/or smug concern of married or coupled-up friends.

Let's face it, these married or coupled-up friends are living with many of the same problems the single woman has walked away from.

Single women are not inherently missing some secret ingredient that might explain why they are alone. Some women choose it for their reasons. For others, they repeatedly stumble in love. Perhaps the single girl has become so independent and self-sufficient she struggles to tolerate the natural ups and downs that show up in every relationship. She's a bit impatient. Either way, she is figuring it out alone. In her way and in her time.

The single woman who has passed her thirties is not so easily tamed. Still, most single women (if they're honest!) dream of finding that love, although not all. We are not a monolithic entity. This book is for the single woman who does want that forever soul mate love but is no longer prepared to abandon herself for it. She will pray for it and wish for it, but she will not sit around waiting for it. The single woman is a survivor. She is driven, resourceful, and on purpose. And by god, she is smart, and good lord, she is sexy.

We love men; we want men; we need men, and we ladies aren't for the turning. We need to learn to love ourselves first. Men aren't that complicated; they need clear signals from us about what we want. That way, they can decide if they wish to give it or not. And we can determine if we will take what he offers. See, two adults making rational decisions about their mutual futures.

We want a good old-fashioned love story. The one with the strong leading man, the one who supports, protects, and worships us.

Now, The Pussycat Dolls can sing, "I don't need a man" all they want, but if you're a heterosexual woman, then you do. You want one, you need one, and whenever you let your imagination explore

> *I am a woman in love*
>
> *And I do anything*
>
> *To get you into my world*
>
> *And hold you within*
>
> *It's a right I defend*
>
> *Over and over again*
>
> *- Barbra Streisand*

the possibility of this fine brotha' stepping into your life, you get very excited about the prospect of having one. Don't cha?! Yes, of course, you do. It's only natural.

I don't care if you're a Victoria Secret model, or earning a million pounds a month, if you've visited the peak of Machu Picchu and found your inner guru, or if you're the first female engineer at NASA, once you close your doors at the end of a long successful or otherwise day, the reality hits you. No one to share all your fabulousness with you. No one to kill the spider, fix the broken fuse, watch box sets, or wait for you to put the kids to bed. It's the little things that matter. No amount of success in a woman's life can replace the love and warmth of a good man. And if you think it can, this book is not for you.

The structure and support available to a woman in a healthy marriage or intimate relationship is an excellent boost to her mental health. Please don't let anyone tell you any different. Look, a romantic relationship is one of the four pillars of life. The others are health, friends/family, and spiritual connection/purpose. Think of the cornerstones of life as the legs of a chair, each component being crucial to your happiness.

The single woman may have had quite a few failed relationships under her Hermes belt, but she's still excited. And you know why? Because with every goodbye, she has learned new lessons about herself and about love. That is why we are on this planet. It's a journey of self-development. Personal growth and enlightenment. It's a solitary pursuit. And the single woman has VIP access to this spiritual journey. That's why I emphasize using the single time wisely.

Still, she desires to be loved. She might talk about love a lot. It's as if it makes her deficient or desperate or even codependent. Aren't you fed up with people telling you you need to spend time with you, get to know you, *blah, blah, blah* as if every married woman out there has swallowed some self-love, has a Zen bible, and has mastered self-love? Pleeeaaasee! Some of the women I know who are married or in committed relationships are the unhealthiest codependent heifers you'll ever meet.

Truth is, many married women are caught up in repeating unhealthy patterns in love, just like the single woman. The difference is it's happening within the confines of their marriages. They're just not telling you about it. My single girls don't get it twisted. There's nothing wrong with you. It's called the human condition.

> *"I will not sulk about having no boyfriend, but develop inner poise and authority and sense of self as woman of substance, complete without boyfriend, as best way to obtain boyfriend."*
>
> *- Bridget Jones's Diary by Helen Fielding*

A relationship with the right man will enhance your life, bring you joy, security, safety, companionship, and great sex. Who wants to fight against that? Not me, and not you.

Yet, when we say we want to be protected and taken care of, they tell us we're a gold digger or weak if we openly express a desire for love, especially if we want to be a mum or housewife. Women don't seem to need men these days. We can even have babies on our own.

Well, if you're a woman who doesn't need or want a strong, loving, kind man by her side taking care of you, sister, this book is *not* for you. Superwoman is on the top shelf, next aisle down. I suggest you pop that one into your bag instead.

How men think

As we reach the final part of week one, ladies, let us talk about men. You know, those divine yummy creatures who get us all kooky and tingly.

You *must* understand how men think to get the commitment and love you want and deserve. Even a healthy, well-balanced man will misread your signals if you do not spell out that you are not for a casual fling. This time around, you want a loving, healthy relationship with yourself *first*, and then a strong, healthy, loving man to commit to you. These are your new nonnegotiables.

There are two types of women in men's eyes: the one he will marry, and the one he won't. A man will take what you give him. He will treat you as another casual encounter only if you don't spell it out for him. Suppose you are dating and want a commitment. Spell it out from the beginning, and let him meet the kid/s early, too. You need to check him out early and let him see his potential life in front of him.

More than ever, single women are entering relationships without protecting themselves from the pain and damage caused by repeatedly giving themselves to men who do not value them or who have no intentions of committing to them.

You are a queen! The only thing you need to do is let him know you ain't playing. But always (as Steve says) keep it sexy.

You play down your needs in fear of chasing him away. You compromise too much; you don't put your non-negotiables on the table. Worst of all, you just wait and hope he will be on the same page as you. You give him the reins and let him take complete control of the way things will go and cross your fingers and hope he'll want what you want, instead of just spelling it out to him.

> To us, your power comes from one simple thing: you 're a woman, and we men will do anything humanly possible to impress you so that, ultimately, we can be with you. You 're the driving force behind why we wake up every day. Men go out and get jobs and hustle to make money because of women. We drive fancy cars because of women. We dress nice, put on cologne, get haircuts and try to look all shiny and new for you. We do all of this because the more our game is stepped up, the more of you we get. You 're the ultimate prize.
>
> - Steve Harvey
>
> Act Like a Lady, Think Like a Man

It took me a while to understand that I would never adopt myself out for mistreatment again. That I must hold on to me and take full responsibility for me and my well-being and choices in love.

Before getting to this place, it often takes a woman to go through a lot of pain, rejection, denial, resistance to facing herself. Some women cannot change; they are incapable of this recovery's rigorous honesty. They cannot look at themselves, are too headstrong, and refuse to admit they have a problem.

But I think you're ready. Remember, we seek progress, not perfection. Just as long as you are growing, you are winning. No matter how small the increments.

Congratulations. You have reached the end of week one. You have learned that you have a problem with self-love and where the root of your problem stems from. Let us move on to week two, which is all about renewed hope and recovering a sense of identity.

However bad your relationships have been, however long you've been single, there is hope. It doesn't matter. Once you have gone through these twelve steps, you will be ready for love. True, committed, sexy love. And believe me, you will get it.

This week we learn to admit there is a problem, that we have lost power in our relationships; that we have sold ourselves short; but never forget how powerful you are, as you walk your road towards greater wholeness, glowing your feelings to come up and giving them the space they require to show you the areas within you that need healing.

Have fun, be bold, do you your way, and most of all, don't forget. Keep it sexy!

> *"Sometimes we motivate ourselves*
> *by thinking of what we want to become*
> *other times we motivate ourselves*
> *by thinking about who we*
> *don't ever want to be again."*
>
> – Shayne Niemeyer

The Big Takeaways

- **Feel the vibrations:** You attract what you are feeling inside

- **Mirror Mirror:** Your Relationships are a blessing. They mirror your relationship with yourself and what areas need more love and attention.

- **In all in your head:** You can change the neurological imprint that drives you towards limiting beliefs in love.

- **The single woman:** The priority is to reclaim power over yourself not men.

- *For some Women, getting into a relationship means losing power.* - *A childhood where caregivers couldn't attune to your needs leaves you with a deficit in your relationships.*

- *Self-awareness is the big business:* *Recovering Self-love and your personal power can only happen when you being you put your first.*

- *Forget stocks and shares. Invest in yourself is the new Bloomberg:* *Become your own best friend. Get a therapist or a coach to work through unresolved childhood issues.*

- *Love you and he will come:* *Nothing is more important than your relationship with yourself. Extraordinary relationships start with you.*

- **Self-Control Please:** *No sex before commitment IF you want commitment.*

- **Lip Control Pease:** *No kiss until date four or five.*

- **Get a life - control please:** No waiting around, neglecting him.

Step 2

HOPE

Recovering your Authentic Self

There's a hole in my bucket

In step one, we admitted we were powerless in our relationships, that we gave a disproportionate amount of our power, time, and energy away to the men we loved.

Whether you were chasing them, trying to make them love you, trying to keep them committed, abandoning yourself to avoid rejection, settling for less or simply waiting for some man to bring the excitement and aliveness your life lacks, you sought companionship and relationship with him above relationship with yourself.

This chapter is to educate you about where limiting beliefs about yourself originated. And the secret to why you have certain expectations when you get into romantic relationships that prevent you from evolving beyond old patterns in love.

The limiting beliefs you have about yourself, can cause you to give away your power and abandon yourself in relationships.

Week 2

This week you reclaim your Authentic Self by dis-identifying with your limiting beliefs

From the earliest years you may have traded your right to be authentic, for the love and approval of parents, siblings and others.

This meant in adulthood your relationship suffered, as you put the needs of others before your own or manipulated others to get love.

You did not realise that you do not have to do one single thing to be worthy of another's love, time and commitment. You did not know that you are lovable and deserving just the way you are.

The songs, quotes and tips, are aimed at empowering you into reclaiming your authentic self.

As step by step, you begin to claim your right to give and receive love from a place of authenticity.

This week you reclaim your throne Queen. You fall madly in love with you, releasing all limiting beliefs surrounding your value and worth.

This week use prayer to tap into the unconditional love that surrounds you, you say, "I allow love to pour into my life like never before!"

Now take a deep breath, channel Lizzo and repeat after me 3 times

"That bitch in the mirror like yeah, I'm in love

Love, love, love, love, love, love (In love)

Like yeah, I'm in love

Love, love, love (In love)

Look up in the mirror like damn she the one"

I gave away my power in many ways and for various reasons. I couldn't seem to help it. Sure, I succeeded in other areas of my life, and when I was single, I was a girl on fire. Enter hot man, and suddenly, I am distracted from myself and not so self-assured.

I used to be so confused by that. Like what is that? Without my man du jour, it seems there was a loneliness I just couldn't shake off! More like an incompleteness, accompanied by a secret question about my worth and value; am I enough, will he really choose me, will he really want to stay with me?

Without someone by my side, I sensed that something crucial was missing from my life. How come others find someone and partner with them, I'd ask myself sitting in front of my TV stuffing my face with chocolate, watching yet another episode of Finding Anna or Married at First sight load up, and by now it's well after midnight. I'm not peaceful, I'm distracted and feeling incomplete.

Perhaps you walk around carrying a conviction as heavy as your Sainsbury's Christmas shop, that a relationship, and perhaps children will fulfil you. I know I did.

These feelings can be debilitating, and hold you back in life, keeping you I'll at ease and using addictions to keep you from feeling too much. Think, if you believe you need someone or something else to make you complete, it will affect your enthusiasm, energy and life choices in detrimental ways. Without you even being aware.

One way such debilitating beliefs show up is that you might not have the self-belief to fully step into your purpose.

> Love yourself first because that's who you'll be spending the rest of your life with!"
>
> –Les Brown

If you have a belief, whether conscious or unconscious that you are not complete, without your 'other half,' then how can you possibly be firing on all cylinders in your career. How can you then summon the energy to lead a powerful, exciting, and autonomous life to discover you.

Until now, you might have been seeking from your relationships with others, which can be found only within a relationship with yourself first. It took em a long time to figure that out.

Occasionally, when you get still enough, for long enough, you are in touch with a deeper awareness there is inner healing to be done. That something in you feels broken or disconnected. That something just isn't right and is holding you back from true fulfilment.

Still, seeking love and validation from men, craving the excitement love brings, getting all wrapped up in the drama and distraction from ourselves is usually what takes precedence over doing the self-love work required to live truly fulfilled and exciting lives.

Relationships and romantic love are God's highest gift to us. Being in love with a sexy king of a man is pure delicious. A romantic relationship with the right person, has the power to heal childhood wounds, and revive dreams and passions lying dormant on the seabed of your heart. The right person can provide a sense of safety, belonging and contentment that is inexplicable.

Romantic relationships can be the most powerful healing, renewing and containing spaces our lives will ever know, and a place from which we can flourish into our highest selves.

I mean, check this, our romantic relationships offer us opportunities for personal growth and building our emotional resilience we simply can't find in therapy, coaching or anywhere else, not even loving by ourselves and cultivating self-love can we access the level of growth, passion, excitement and safety a romantic relationship can offer. This is why we get so kooky about love.

But wait. There is an order to everything. A romantic relationship can *never* fulfil you if you haven't got a relationship with yourself, that is solid and dynamically set up to soothe you and generate love and safety from within, with no validation or stimulus needed from ousted of yourself - you can sooth and stabilise yourself. You get me?

It is imperative you build this inner *structure,* to hold you upright, when love triggers your old wounds and sets off a sequence of difficult events in your relationships.

You must first *learn* how to fulfil yourself, by cultivating a kind, mentoring, intimate, forgiving and loving relationship with the most important person in your life; that's right, you got it, girl, you got it! What? No! I'm not talking about Chris Brown! I'm talking about you, silly...

Only you can fix the hole in your bucket - *It's not Henry's job!*

If you don't cultivate a loving relationship with *you* before embarking on a beautiful journey with another, then falling in love for you will always be like pouring water into a bucket with tiny holes at the bottom. Each time you try to fill it up, it just keeps emptying itself.

Do you remember the old song 'there's a hole in my bucket?' Listen to it, it's a wonderful song and it's very funny. I think it has many meanings about love and relationships, as well as gender stereotypes, but for me, it's significant how we search for others to fix the holes in our buckets and get exasperated with them when they can't fix the things in is that have been hurting or wounded for a very long time.

We often don't even know these holes are there, how they got there, or anything about them in our relationships. Still, they show up in the needs, demands, expectations we have from our partners, or relationships.

We go around looking for love in all the wrong places. That's one way of looking at it. I don't believe in wrong places, only right paces that lead us to where we need to be. Never judge or criticise yourself. You are right where you're meant to be.

When we have these holes in our bucket it feels like all the love that you're giving isn't reciprocated. Or you can't trust. Or be yourself, or say what you feel, or attract or hang onto love, or you're afraid of it, or you don't believe you are enough to give or receive love.

You see, all these feelings, doubts, insecurities, fears, represent those tiny holes in the bottom of your bucket. They have to be filled up before you can 'hold' the blessings, healing and excitement love is trying to bring to you.

> There's a hole in my bucket
>
> Dear Liza, dear Liza.
>
> There's a hole in my bucket,
>
> Dear Liza, a hole.
>
> Then fix it, dear Henry,
>
> Dear Henry, dear Henry.
>
> Then fix it, dear Henry,
>
> Dear Henry, fix it.

If your bucket has those holes in it, you will never have the love you want and deserve and you cannot expect your lover to mend these holes. It is not their job. It is your job. If you find love before mending these holes, you will destroy it, or it will forever elude you. Your relationship will be strained, inauthentic, lack depth, communication and intimacy. So, let's get plugging girls. Time waits for no man!

All right, so how on earth do you plug up the little bitches at the bottom of your bucket, you ask. And I commend you on such a well-worded question.

The answer is this, get to know yourself intimately. That is the first step toward becoming a hole-less bucket, if you know what I mean.

Get to know your triggers, your unresolved issues and precisely who you are bringing into your relationships, you will be unable to benefit from the miracles of love, just like that bucket I described earlier, your relationship will not keep replenishing and renewing itself. It will get stuck.

If love hasn't been working for you, if you've been cheated on, left, not chosen, or push men away, avoid love or are a woman hardened by fear of rejection, then you are exactly in the right place. I had so much drama, pain and suffering in my romantic relationships for at least two decades of my life. I was often confused, lost, afraid and didn't have my own back. I didn't know how to love me or value myself.

So, here's the thing, something has to give if you are to get the love you deserve. To attract a man who is powerful, handsome, intelligent, kind, considerate, available, sexy, (that's my list, what's yours?), first you need to tap into the excitement power, sexiness, goodness and energy that comes with falling deeply in love with you.

Falling in love with yourself is the secret to attracting love. Falling in love with you, is beyond any good feeling you can get from another. If you are serious about finding and sustaining romantic love. The journey *must* start with you. But first, we need a bit of education about where these issues in love started with you, and precisely what steps to take to turn things around.

As little girls, we may have been denied the opportunity to fully be ourselves, that is, we may not have been not allowed to be willful and difficult, angry or stubborn. We could not be as demanding and moody or emotional because our caregivers may have been too preoccupied, depressed or fragile to give us the room we needed to develop all sides of our forming personality.

> "You'll learn, as you get older, that rules are made to be broken. Be bold enough to live life on your terms, and never, ever apologize for it. Go against the grain, refuse to conform, take the road less traveled instead of the well-beaten path. Laugh in the face of adversity, and leap before you look. Dance as though EVERYBODY is watching. March to the beat of your own drummer. And stubbornly refuse to fit in."
>
> — Mandy Hale, The Single Woman: Life, Love, and a Dash of Sass

This meant we had to become attuned to *their* demands, sensing we had to comply to be tolerated and loved, or at least interpreting it that way,

We learned that NOT expressing our authentic feelings and needs kept us safe. We learned that authenticity could cause rejection. and so, we started hiding who we really were and how we really felt, for the love and approval of others, this led us to develop a *false self*. While there are different levels of falseness in self, the main characteristic is being disconnected from one's aliveness and spontaneity.

British psychoanalyst Dr Donald Winnicott advanced the theory of a true self and a false self in a series of papers in the 1960s. Winnicott contends that everyone is divided into these two selves, and that people develop a false self to protect their inner, more vulnerable true self.

Winnicott points out that having a very strong False Self persona keeps people from acting according to their spontaneity and creative impulses, leaving them feeling unoriginal and empty, sometimes with very little idea of why they feel this way. Now, this is one little hole in your bucket

Growing into young women with this false self persona, no matter how hard we tried - our relationships seemed to involve a particular set of insecurities and anxieties.

When we met someone and developed feelings, our thoughts, behaviours, and assumptions repeatedly created and attracted negative and painful experiences. These things became our love constellation.

Your 'love constellation 'is the sum of feelings, thoughts and actions that drive your thinking to galvanise you into a toxic love experience. A combination of a false self, limiting core beliefs and low self-esteem mean you have been creating bad relationships for yourself.

> I would have given you all of my heart, but there's someone whose torn it apart, and its taken just all that I have but if you want I'll try to love again. Baby I'll try to love again but I know. The first cut is the deepest..
>
> – Rod Stewart

Tip;

The definition of a toxic relationship is that push and pull dynamic. One minute you're in, then you're out.

Your love constellation is the specific way your negative beliefs about yourself formed in childhood plays out or constellates in your relationships. It is your attachment style, your love language; It is how you behave, what you expect, or *what happens to you* when you develop romantic feelings for someone.

In her book, a journey from abandonment to healing, Susan Anderson gives us some insight into some causes behind our childhood trauma or hurts;

An abandonment wound can be formed in a variety of unsuspecting and more obvious ways:

- Birth trauma (separation at birth, c-section birth, incubators)
- Being dropped off at summer camp
- Being dropped off at Grandma's house for a night when you're little
- Boarding school

- Divorced parents

- An absent parent

- A sick parent

- Death of a parent

- A close family member dying

- Growing up in an emotionally cold environment where it wasn't safe to express yourself

- Childhood abuse, sexual abuse, or verbal insults

- Emotionally aloof or distant parents.

These are just some experiences, helpfully outlined by Susan, that will form negative core beliefs in a child's brain, which later show up in your adult relations and constellation around particular events: Beliefs-like. I'm not lovable, I've been abandoned, something must be wrong with me, the world isn't safe, I can't trust love, I have to do everything alone, I'm only lovable if I behave a certain way" or "I have to do X to be loved," and so on.

If you experienced any hurt, rejection, or neglect like this in childhood, which, let's face it, is most of us. Love will not be so easy for you until you address these problems. This is because you may have formed some very damaging core beliefs about yourself.

These negative, false beliefs will be eating away at your ability to love and accept yourself and others, so there may be a lack of trust, an abundance of fear, defences against rejection featuring as the main villain at the centre of your love story.

> The difference between feeling yourself in action, here and now, and visualising yourself in action, as though you were in a motion picture movie screen, is the difference between success and failure.
>
> –Neville Goddard

Your negative core beliefs about yourself and love are likely to be unconscious, festering just beneath the level of your conscious thoughts, thwarting your attempts at self-love and acceptance.

Meet your Love Constellation; the dangerous process that blocks you from giving and receiving love?

First, many of your negative beliefs about yourself are not operating at a conscious level. They exist beneath the level of your conscious awareness and influence how you express and receive love.

We've all heard of the 5 love languages, well, think of your 'love constellation,' as a love language on steroids. Your love constellation wraps itself around your limiting core beliefs and sets in motion a sequence of internal and external events that keep you looked in false beliefs about yourself and your relationships.

It is imperative to remember that love is a learned response, a learned reaction, we have a template that tells us what love is, and what we should give and receive when we love. Until we liberate ourselves from that childhood template and learn who we are in love and how to become a woman who knows herself well enough to avoid triggered reactions and acting out.

When you learn about your own love constellation, what activates it and how it plays out in your relationships you can discover how to give and receive love more effectively; you can discover the missing

> Giving and receiving love is at the centre of every single adult's sense of well-being
>
> –The 5 Love languages
>
> Gary Chapman

ingredient in some of your past relationships and you can learn how to build powerful, communicative and mutually loving relationships.

So, what exactly is your love constellation?

The word constellation refers to a group of stars or people gathered together.

What happens to the stars when under the influence of certain forces also happens inside of us when we are under the influence of certain forces. Forces such as love and relationships.

Remember, a love constellation is a particular *form or pattern that* your emotions take whenever you feel threatened in your relationships. By feeling threatened, I mean, whenever your core belief about yourself feels like it is coming true.

Oh, if you have unaddressed negative core beliefs about love, you will make them come true. Just sayin'.

Core Beliefs as Self-fulfilling Prophecy

If you believe it, it will come true

Your core belief will be something like "I am not smart", "I must work hard to be worthy of love," or "If I am to keep the love I must be constantly over giving of myself."

Following these negative core beliefs, your feelings will become triggered whenever anything in your relationships seems to mirror these beliefs, like you attract someone who always expects you to do everything; then your thoughts will take this as concrete evidence and expand on these beliefs, which will look something like;

> Everything you believe affects everything that comes to you
>
> –Abraham Hicks

Because I am not smart and must work hard to be worthy of love, and constantly over give if I am to keep love or my relationships, I must do all the work and take all the responsibility for everything. If I do not do this, I will not be loved and will be alone. Therefore, "I am the girl who has no intrinsic value."

There is a shift from a negative belief about yourself as an individual, to a negative belief about yourself *in* relation to another. Your love constellation dictates you are the "girl who has no intrinsic value."

In the eyes of another, no longer just the girl who is unlovable or unworthy you may have felt in childhood.

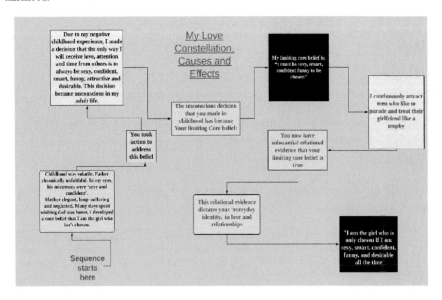

Diagram 1

Use the above diagram, to see if you can work out of your own constellations from childhood to adulthood. Remember, there are many constellations or patterns formed from our childhood experiences- not just one.

Are you the girl who is always abandoned or 'the one who gets cheated on.' Maybe you're the girl who always takes care of everythingor always pays for everything.

Maybe you're 'the girl who always settles for less' or never dares say how she *really* feels. Whatever you feel you are in relationships with others, this belief has its root in the negative core belief you have about yourself from your early years.

Now, have a good look at diagram 2, below. It is an example from the love constellation of Valerie, a client.

Notice how the little girl who was hurt in her childhood, made the false and dangerous decision that she had to work hard for love to address the shortcomings of her parents and siblings.

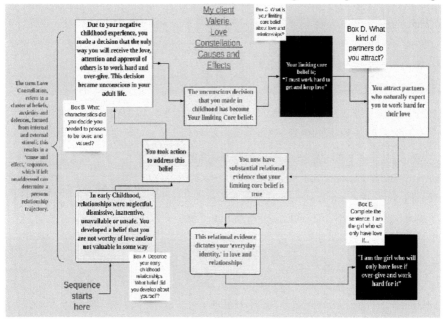

Diagram 2

This is a terrible double bind. You are *creating* the very relationship you are trying so hard to avoid, which leaves you with a deep sense of injustice, throwing your hand up and asking God or yourself questions like "why is this happening to me?" but bad relationships never *just happen to you*, they can only happen *through you*. You create your bad relationships with the unconscious limited beliefs you hold about yourself! You create them because you are over-identified with the past, and deep down it's likely that much like me, you are deeply afraid of loving and being hurt.

And so, you sit at the bottom, your well-cultivated emotional and familial system, a system that feeds you disempowered beliefs like, you never get chosen. Or you always get cheated on, or you aren't good enough to be loved, or you'd better not speak your truth, or he'll leave, etc. All false beliefs block you from giving and receiving love. If you have these beliefs, you will only attract men who will fulfil your negative beliefs about yourself.

Today, I see how my bad relationships happened through me, in others' words, how I created them according to my unconscious limited beliefs. I would often cry myself to sleep wondering why the married man I was dating or the workaholic

I was in love with, or the man still raw from his divorce "didn't choose me." Can you see how our core beliefs unconsciously drive us to make them a reality? It's like seeing sold houses and getting totally devastated when you can't move in.

It's kind of insane. If I wanted to be chosen, surely I would get with an available man, right? Wrong, our unconscious limited beliefs are super powerful and will drive out behaviour until we expose these beliefs to the light and kill them off forever!

It is a painful cycle, nevertheless, one I lived with for many, many years. But there is value in this repetitive, seemingly impenetrable loop. With every goodbye, we get more self-aware. More understanding, more self-compassionate.

We get to release this old identity and these stubborn patterns stored in our bodies as our younger traumatised selves. After years of training our chemistry and biology to respond to love with desperation, anxiety, fear, and insecurity, we get to reverse this process.

> Everything depends on our attitude towards ourselves . That which we will not affirm as true of ourselves cannot develop in our life.
>
> —Neville Goddard

Step 2 is where we begin our crossover, from allowing our child self to run our love show to choosing the conscious adult, and putting her firmly back behind the wheel. FYI little girls are not allowed to drive!

Here, in step 2, we acknowledge the failures of our parents and the pain and trauma they caused. And then we press on to greener pastures.

Notice how it all starts with the little girl, making a decision that can mess up the rest of your life in both diagrams.

The little girl still holding onto her hurts and wounds does not get to decide about who loved you and who didn't. Or precisely what was going on with your parents and siblings. As with all children, her ability to understand grown-up life is impaired.

Adult lives are complicated, people have affairs for many reasons, but my father was very faithful to me until he died. I can see as an adult how much I meant to him. Children should not be expected to make adult decisions.

We also see how the little girl in Valerie's diagram was still very much controlling her life until Valerie came to therapy to release it and reclaim her adult self as the leading lady of her life.

We equally acknowledge that we have feared changing, that we have built a mindset that shapes our reality and relationships to accommodate an old wound - around our traumatised child identity.

And so, now we see things more clearly; our behaviour in love makes more sense. The veil is lifting, and we see how we were the source of our own experiences. We see how we created the very thing we were trying to avoid.

We now step into a new consciousness, no longer allowing the wounded child consciousness to drive us but to make a symbolic crossing over into our adult selves. This new sight and awareness is LIT, and it will change everything!

Now try creating your own love constellation in diagram 3 below. Just fill in the empty boxes.

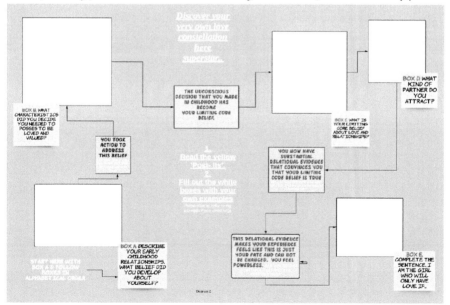

Diagram 3

Now, take a deep breath, channel the Black Crowes and repeat after me three times.

> *I'm seeing things for the first time.*
>
> *I'm seeing things for the first time.*
>
> *I'm seeing things for the first time.*
>
> *In my life..*
>
> *In my life..*
>
> *Yeah!*

Superbly done! Now, we have that out of our system. We can set sail on our unstoppable journey, back home to ourselves, where true love, authenticity, intimacy and relationships await! Ahoy Captain!

Your little Girl - Take time to know her

This deepening of your relationship with your child self will transform your romantic relationships. Heck, it will transform your whole freakin' life.

There is a little girl in you, that was hurt and wounded in childhood. She continues to hold on to that wounding, and when she is triggered, she hijacks the tone and mood of your relationships as quickly as you can say whatever did happen to Baby Jane?!

And then, girl, your relationships are in serious jeopardy. Especially the one you have with yourself. Lookout! is it a bird, is it a plane? No, it's Self-abandonment. Duck!

This is what my little girl looks like in real time!

"Hey hun, how was your day?" Oh, how I love this man, I think as he shrugs off his coat and hangs it on the wall hooks. He smiles like only he can.

"It was really good, oh, and I'm doing some work with that really talented photographer I told you about."

"What photographer?" I say, bewildered, pouring hot water onto a sweetly fragranced herbal teabag. "I don't remember you telling me about that," I say with a smile, now sipping my herbal tea, feeling blissful and relaxed.

> Most of us are totally unaware that our inner conversation are the causes of the circumstances in our lives
>
> —Neville Goddard

"You know, " he says," the one from New York."

Suddenly, I feel a jolt in my abdomen, as if I have been punched. I am no longer in my adult self, nor am I in the present moment here. I have collapsed into a seven-year-old whose father was chronically unfaithful and witnessed many arguments and violence around infidelity between her parents. I continue.

"You mean the one with the big tits? " I snort aggressively. He frowns and throws me an irritated look. "What? "

Oh, but I'm ready for him. A gun is positively off the safety. "What do you mean, what"? "Are you deaf? I said, the one with the big TITS!" I'm offline. Slightly frantic, heart pounding, adrenaline and cortisol flooding through my body. I AM the little girl. I am entirely out of my frontal cortex and in fight or flight.

One marker of relational trauma is an inability to stay in the present moment without being hijacked into an old wound as if it were happening right here and now. Attachment trauma steals your present and freedom to love and enjoy your partner in the present.

This is because he mentioned he is excited to be working with a talented photographer. There is no need to mistrust him, no reason to doubt him - Still, this is what *happens*. *Trauma is a powerful force that destroys relationships. We must, Recognise this and release the hold it has on us?*

Have you ever noticed how when you get hurt, rejected, overwhelmed, or disappointed by your man, you collapse into that traumatised child self?. Can you think of ways this has happened to you in your relationships? Remember, look for the similarities and not the differences.

There I was, chilling in the kitchen. So, at peace and in love. The book! Gone is the woman at peace with her man, the woman who feels good about herself and feels safe in her environment and body.

And just like any good old Broadway show, enter, stage left, the 'little girl 'panic. All your little girl feelings of being unworthy and not enough and fear of abandonment come rushing to the surface.

The only problem is, now, an adult sitting in front of the man you love being hijacked by a 5-year-old on a mission to destroy!

According to Dr. Audrey Sherman, licensed psychologist, coach, and the author of the book 'Dysfunction Interrupted-How to Quickly Overcome Depression, Anxiety and Anger Starting Now,' this demonic-like possession takes place because your brain developed coping mechanisms designed to protect you

Our brains develop coping mechanisms, such as distrust not to be hurt again. Or anxiety, to be watchful for the same reasons. Our brains teach us to develop strategies for hanging on to people so we won't be left alone. I will add that our brains develop strategies to push people away before they do it to us.

She explains that such fear and elevated emotions are altered states, taking us out of alignment.

> "Experience has taught us that we have only one enduring weapon in our struggle against mental illness: the emotional discovery and emotional acceptance of the truth in the individual and unique history of our childhood."
>
> –Alice Miller, The Drama of the Gifted Child: T — he Search for the True Self

Our brains get stuck believing that our safety is sourced outside of ourselves because it much *is* the case in childhood. When we are small, we depend on others for our very survival. A baby will literally die without its mother's love, attention, and touch. Our safety, sense of self, and ability to love ourselves are in other people as children.

Our brains do not recognise whether these strategies are helpful for us in the long run. Coping mechanisms are developed out of fear.

Understanding this is critical to your well-being. It means you get to gain insight into the actual starting point of your current emotional difficulties. This allows you to trace a thread forward to why you're where you are today.

As a child, you couldn't do much to escape your distress, but as an adult, you can conquer it by understanding its roots and putting it in its place.

When these childhood feelings are triggered in your adult romantic relationships, they can hit you and the relationship like a sledgehammer.

At times, these feelings are disproportionate to the matter at hand. Maybe he didn't call, or you suspect him of cheating because he forgot to take his phone off silent mode, or he's not available to you the way you'd him. So, in response to these disappointments, you might begin to catastrophize or panic or go into withdrawal or manic fix-it mode.

Whatever you do, you feel wounded at a visceral level. It is essential to acknowledge that you are *reacting, not responding*. You are reacting from an old wound. Until we release our traumas, we will always be reactive to our relationships.

You feel this 'child self 'inside your adult body so powerfully, on a somatic level—your nervous system pushes out chemicals, pounding heart, shortness of breath.

In a blink of an eye, you feel you can't trust the man you thought was your best friend or withdraw from someone you speak to every day. Your wounds are driving this acting out.

But you can break this pattern, and you will!

It's high time to de-weaponise your little girl. Stop her from launching those time travel missiles that propel you out of your present and into your past.

Loving your inner child helps you remember your innocence and recognise how much life loves you. Ask the child within , what can I do for you today?

—Louise Hay

There comes a time when the child needs to know her place, lovingly, of course. The little girl has been running your show until now. When you fall in love, she's been sabotaging you with her unconscious narrative of unworthiness. A little girl should NOT be dating.

Now, let me elaborate here. The wounded part within you, the little girl is still holding onto the hurts from her past. She believes in the messages she picked up in childhood. Messages she is not important, lovable, or enough. Messages she had better be kind, quiet, pretty, a good cook, a good fuck, a good mum, funny, smart or perfect, if she expects someone to love her, to choose her to go with through this life.

Those who have experienced trauma, neglect, or abuse in our childhood usually grow without an instinctive drive towards self-love and protection. We lack awareness of how to give and receive love without hurting ourselves.

And so, we say goodbye to this old way of relating. Time to step into your power and anchor into the woman you are today, into a future that looks very different from anything in your past. And that future will need to involve a God of your understanding.

A God of your understanding.

Many of us have made men our higher power. This was a grave mistake. The purpose of our connection to source is to be yolked to our authentic selves. When we are deeply close to our higher power, we are in true alignment and can accomplish anything we desire.

By making men our higher power, we forgot that the only true soulmate we have is ourselves. We are the only ones who can rescue ourselves from pain, and the only ones who can lift our lives to unimaginable heights. Only us. No man can ever give you the happiness you seek. We hoped that they would remove our fear and help us to love ourselves. We relied on them to take care of us.

Unconsciously, we wrestled with them to become the parents we never had; Some tried, some resisted, but all failed. Men were never meant to compensate for the parenting we never had. That's God's job. It is also not the job of our men to heal the wounds of our childhoods. All roads lead to a God of your understanding for healing and transformation.

The power that made us has given us a choice to create our lives and choose the thoughts we think. These men were the greatest gift we could ever hope to have because it means we have the power to create the lasting love we have always dreamed of. First, though, we have to love ourselves.

The closest organised religion I identify with is Christianity. I do not attend church regularly, nor is my style of prayer rooted in any traditional theology. I love Christ and I love the power that is almighty God. Sometimes I prayer with scripture, sometimes I just talk.

> Stop believing in God and start believing as God
>
> –Neville Goddard

I do not pray according to a set of rules. At the core of my Fatih is a deep love and respect for my higher power, I call him and I refer to him as God. You must find your sacred connection. Whatever it is for you, the universe.

Your higher self. Your angels. Find what works for you. And remember, don't be put off by what I believe, do you!! Look for the similarities in our stories and not the differences.

The bible suggests to us;

"Seek ye first the kingdom of God, and all else shall be added unto you."

When you seek God first, you shall have all your heart's desires if these desires are indeed for your highest good.

Another way to look at this is to think I must seek myself first. I must have my first attention. All else will be added to my life.

In AA, they say, whatever you put before recovery, you lose. The principle here is the same. Take care of yourself first, and then miracles happen.

Time to cross over. This 'crossing over 'process requires that you become acquainted with a God of your understanding. Whether you call it Source, a Higher power, or Higher Self, whatever you prefer to call it is up to you, but making that connection is vital to your life now.

Making a connection to the God of your understanding is at the heart of this step. It will lead you to cross over from relying on self-will and ego to depending on self in relationships with a loving higher consciousness. This shift is vital if we attract, build and create safe and healthy relationships going forward.

To have a relationship with the omnipresent higher intelligence within (and outside of you) will guide you to anchor into becoming a woman who holds the source of her value, healing, worth, and power within herself—no longer seeking these things from the men she loves. Or any source outside of herself.

God (which is what I prefer to call him, encompassing masculine and feminine energies) is different things to different people.

For me, God is that magnificent, loving force that presides over us all, that still small voice within that encourages you to keep going when you lose faith, choose peace over drama, or love over lust. Self-control over self-destruction.

> *Nothing comes from without*
> *All things come from within.*
> – Neville Goddard

That loving force that shows up in your life with little and big miracles, that extra money that shows up just when you thought you were out of cash. That best friend that calls just when you felt unloved, that encouraging note to yourself you find in the draw, just when you think no one is on your side.

God is how I feel after a run, when I finish a beloved creative project, when the sun shines on my face when I hold my daughter in my arms, and when I am so filled with feelings of love, peace, and acceptance that everything is perfect. These are a few moments when I feel God. For me, God is pure love and pure peace.

These days, most of us are familiar with the concept of God or a higher power. When I speak of crossing over in this chapter, I am talking about shifting from ego mind to an inner consciousness, which has a higher power at its centre.

Many of us are walking around blindly identified with our egos. Feelings of fear, doubt, unworthiness, and scarcity all come from the ego.

If we genuinely wish to find new and more profound ways to love ourselves and others, we will need to detach from ego, which is the mind, and attach to the deeper presence within us. To start living from a new consciousness and separate from ego living.

Living from a deeper consciousness brings peace and safety and will help you graduate from codependency and self-abandoning behaviours in love.

Now, take a deep breath, Channel Jennifer Hudson.

This week, my lovely, everything will need to slow down in your life so we can pay considerable attention to silence.

Slow down and become more mindful about everything, how you walk, eat, brush your teeth. This transformation starts with the little things, take time to moisturise your skin, go for daily walks or get some exercise, eat well, greens, vegetables, fruits.

Watch less reality TV and listen to less music about looks and material things. Create space to become sensitive to the prompting of the inner voice within, and when prompted, act quickly and follow. Pay considerable attention to your thoughts and replace all doubtful, fearful thoughts with a short prayer or positive affirming thoughts.

A shift will take place in you this week, and you will no longer generate your thoughts from your old story of fear and inadequacy. Hour by hour, and minute by minute, you will reclaim your feminine power. Moving within to receive the love from God, who you can rely on always to meet your needs

> *All you can possibly need or desire is already yours. Call your desires into being by imagining and feeling your wish fulfilled.*
>
> –Neville Goddard

Your relationship with your higher power will teach you how to love yourself, but you need to get into an intimate relationship with him first. Slow down and let it develop. Let him know you, tell him everything you've ever wanted your man to listen to and show interest in.

Talk to God about your hopes, dreams, family, disappointments, and heartaches. It will seem odd to those who do not already have faith in God but opening a dialogue with your higher power is essential to your transformation.

When you make your higher power the priority in your life, you automatically make yourself the focus. When you are lonely, depleted, afraid, or feeling inadequate, accept yourself just as you are, and you feel a powerful peace within.

If you feel alive and full of love, creativity, and a complete absence of fear, you are aligned with God.

God's love for you is unconditional. His spirit is that discernible force that resides within and comforts you.

You feel it viscerally, usually within your abdomen. It is a great peace that descends upon you and your thoughts. A more profound intuition you know tells you the right thing, even if that isn't the thing you want to do.

God is constantly reorienting you to turn inwards to find the comfort you seek. God's love is unconditional, non-judgemental, and will replenish and strengthen your time and time again.

With this new orbit, you no longer look to men or to any outside source to provide you with the love and validation you have sought your whole life. You have it all inside of you.

Prayer is highly effective in lowering our reactivity to traumatic and negative events.

–Dr David Spiegal

Through prayer and affirmations, you take action to believe in yourself, love yourself, and surrender to a power greater than you.

Now you can say goodbye to your old story and all the negative limiting beliefs it held about you. This is a radical step. This week you will feel a new power and energy.

Suppose you're not sure how to approach God with this. Start with this prayer.

Dear God,

Until now, I have sought love and validation from men and not from a relationship with you. I have made men my higher power when I should have been seeking you.

My actions have caused me a lot of pain. I am sorry. I have hurt myself and have not sought you. I have been afraid to change because even though giving my power away to men has been painful, it is all I have known. I understand now that you love me unconditionally, and I will surrender to you, accept your love, and seek your guidance.

I commit myself to never giving my power again to the man in my life. My primary goal is to nurture my relationship with you and myself.

I ask you to help me enter an intimate relationship with you. Please help me to find the love and validation I have been seeking from men within myself.

Amen.

Never, ever underestimate the power of prayer. Say this prayer every morning and night before bed.

You will shift from looking outwards for validation to turning inwards for your needs to be met. The first step of your recovery from powerlessness over men is finding your power within.

Quick question;

I know how easy it is to hate him after what he put you through—rejection, lies, deceit, and cruelty. But now, you have shifted from a child to an adult consciousness; you need to take full responsibility for how you showed up in our relationships.

Who knows that you can only attract lasting love when you are clean up your feelings of resentment, victimisation, and blame.

You can never take control of your life from a victimised perspective. Because a victim has no power, all her potential for healing, autonomy, and transformation lies in the perpetrator's actions. She is at his mercy. She is waiting for him to explain, hating him for leaving, mad at him for leaving her alone, expecting him to say sorry. All this leaves you dependent on him for closure.

Prayer is powerful because it focuses you thoughts on something outside of ourselves. During times of stress our nervous system becomes hyper activated and shuts down our executive functioning and prevents us from thinking clearly. When we sit down and focus on prayer, we are able to shift out of this survival mo

de and into a more intentional state.

Dr Hokemeyer

When we take responsibility for what we've experienced and see our part in it, we free ourselves from the bitterness and resentment that binds us to our ex. To release these toxic emotions, we need to stop holding him responsible and figure out our part in the relationship problems—

I gave all my power away to men many, many times. I did not love myself. I didn't know how. After Mum died, there wasn't really any family to lean on, so men and romantic relationships were where I searched for a family type bond.

I waited for my partners to love me because I didn't know how to love myself, protect me, fix me, heal me, and be the attentive, unconditional parents I never had. Unfortunately, no one has perfect parents. No one is perfect.

I tried hard to keep certain men close. The ones I thought I loved. Today I realise they were just the ones who were unavailable.

I beautified myself, cooked, engaged in stimulating intelligent conversation, I was deeply loving and attentive. Spent so much time and energy trying to avoid getting hurt or rejected - it was bloody classic. Looking for love in all the wrong places.

My final toxic relationship was so painful. He was a doctor and he treated me like his patient. Detached, prescriptive and unemotional. I guess he tried a bit, but he was cut out for love on any level.

Looking back now, I can see that is why I chose him, after so much pain and loss, he was a safe option. With him, there would never be anything more than a superficial thing.

I was on the rebound from my daughter's father, we were engaged to be married, but my dreams were crushed when it ended.

I was traumatised and inconsolable by that breakup. I was desperate to have A fun distraction. Instead, I found myself becoming very codependent and self-abandoning with this doctor.

I had deepened my self-awareness exponentially, and learned a lot about loving myself, but I certainly wasn't acting like it. Trauma has a way of regressing us back to very primitive places. Noo worries, though, it's a case of two steps backwards, 1000 steps forward.

After breaking up with this guy, and getting back together many times, I knew I had to get this man out of my life. I wasn't standing for what I need in a relationship. It was awful, cold, lacked communication and was deeply unfulfilling.

I got on my knees and cried and prayed, and my higher power responded and transformed my life. He helped me to focus on what I needed. I wrote this book, focused on what felt good about my life. Running, eating well, coming home to my soul-self.

My creativity, the things that make me feel good about me. Accomplishing things, finishing things, things that give me a sense of my self-esteem, being creative, helping others, fitness nutrition and at the centre of it all is my relationship with God. Oh, how I love him.

Now take a deep breath, channel Dolly Parton and repeat after me.

To know him

Is to love, love, love him.

THE OXFORD LAWYER

The man who brought me to my knees.

Every single romantic relationship, without exception, is a mirror of the relationship you are having with yourself. When you are vulnerable and unable to muster the power to love yourself, you will attract a relationship that mirrors this, a man unable to love you.

When you are lacklustre, without purpose, stuck in fear and afraid to step fully into your life, you will attract a relationship that mirrors this. There is no escape, that is why I say, extraordinary relationships start with you!

I met him in New York. 6.3. Smooth, dark-skinned brother. The way he walked, this understated swagger, eyes in front, soft expression, unassuming.

I remember feeling so utterly unattractive, had gained a lot of weight, and much of my self-esteem was invested in my body image in those days. If my body wasn't banging, I felt I was unlovable, romantically speaking.

I wouldn't dare step foot in the gym unless I wore a waist trainer or some powerful shape wear. I was so ashamed of my body, after having my daughter. I gained 3 stone. Especially as I'd always had a toned, lean body my whole life.

Besides, now hitting my 40s, weight gain happened much easier. My confidence was pretty shot, so when this guy appeared in the same Manhattan bar three days in a row every day, looking like an NBA athlete with that perfectly ripped body, what was I going to do?

Exactly. Absolutely nothing. I didn't look at him. If he went left, I went right. If he walked straight, I walked crooked. If he went to the bar, I remained parched. I went well out of my way to avoid any contact with the man.

I could never have imagined that I would spend the next three years with this man, give him all my power, tolerate his lack of emotional literacy, and his total avoidance of any real intimacy with me. Of course, he had mummy issues, men with such acute emotional avoidance issues always do.

I attracted him because my previous breakup was so painful it launched me into a regression. I became the girl who isn't chosen. That was my childhood narrative, I decided that as Dad was always with a mistress, he didn't choose me/us. I was identified with this falsehood. Naturally, I would attract someone who didn't choose me.

I fell into my old pattern again. Attracted an unavailable man.

It was as if I had a relational *relapse*. *I* was doing so well, the last 10 years, I had Teka to show with a kind, vomited, open and available man. My daughter's dad.

But this one breakup from my daughter's father, sent me running back to old unhealthy places of familiarity and comfort.

> *The only toxic relationship I ever had was the one with myself... everyone else was just. A reflection of that*
>
> –Neha Priya

That's the thing, we start making good progress, attracting healthier people, but if we experience a breakup or some other emotional trauma, we may just have a behavioural relapse.

My point is this, when we experience a relational trauma, we have to be super careful. It is wise to heal before going into another relationship and forget about "get under somebody to get over somebody."

Otherwise, we might find ourselves repeating some of the behaviours we outgrew years ago. Yes, it happens.

Growth is not linear. It is not a thing like, "OK, now I know this, I will never do that again."

Oh no, growth is more like a circular movement, sometimes we have not keep going around and around a thing before we can understand it and soften away from getting involved in dysfunctional relationships.

When trauma happens, we usually default to a regressed, primitive place. We are likely to attract something similar if we are not careful. Perhaps the best we can do is try not to enter a relationship when traumatised. But whatever you do, my lovely, you simply can't lose. Either way, you learn. Now, take a deep breath, channel Alan's Morrisette, and repeat after me three times

> *I recommend getting your heart trampled on to anyone*
> *I recommend walking around naked in your living room*
> *Swallow it down (what a jagged little pill)*
> *It feels so good (swimming in your stomach)*
> *Wait until the dust settles*
> *You live, you learn*
> *You love, you learn*
> *You cry, you learn*
> *You lose, you learn*
> *You bleed, you learn*
> *You scream, you learn*
> *Alanis Morrisett.*

My relationship with the Lawyer was very painful. I pushed and pushed for commitment, for something I don't think I even wanted from him. I was deeply bruised by my former breakup and was looking for a soft place to land.

The constant knocking my head against the wall, the trying to get a commitment from an unavailable man, eventually forced me to turn inward, hold onto myself, and reach for peace and a deeper relationship with my God.

Turns out, the lawyer's complete avoidance of intimacy, forced me into loving myself. Now, how sweet to be loved by me.

So, come on, ladies, you know the drill. Channel Arianna Grande and repeat after me, "I'm so fucking grateful for my ex" can I get an amen.

I'd have to say that the period of my life when I met the lawyer, was perhaps amongst the worst time I've ever had in my life; suddenly a single mother, an ensuing bitter separation, two step-children that hate my guts, and a tiny baby who needs me to love and protect her. All this when I could hardly breathe from the impact of this loss. Luckily for me, my daughter gave me all I needed to love again. She was, and still is my sunshine through it all.

The lawyer was a rebound. I tried to turn it into a relationship, but I knew I could never with a man who didn't value emotional closeness and communication. I was broken down and vulnerable from my last real relationship.

He was incredibly friendly, and we sat and chatted. He told me all about his impressive accomplishments. He had my attention.

A few weeks in, and I visit his house. He's showing me around and announces the master bedroom, which we walk into: big room, nice, whatever.

He opens the door to the walk-in closet, and I'm like, "what the"... The back wall of the closet is full of women's clothes. Loads of plastic storage boxes on the floor filled with make-up and women stuff.

Honestly, I'm shocked. He told me he and his wife separated a while back, and she'd moved out a long time ago. So, why were her clothes still here? I felt like someone had punched me in the stomach. We were getting closer, and now I discover that his house is full of the ghosts of his wife.

> Sometimes you gotta put aside what you feel for them and pay attention to what their actions are saying they feel for you
>
> –Anonymous

Still, I stayed. And so did the clothes. You can see a pattern forming of how I allowed myself and my needs to diminish slowly. I want to feel cherished, special, like the only girl in the world. Yet, I did honour what I know I deserve. I allowed the way I want to feel in a relationship just disappear in the 4 walls of a walk-in wardrobe.

At first, I wasn't so bothered, as I was genuinely grateful for a distraction from the pain of my breakup and losing my family.

But I felt hurt seeing this still very active attachment to his wife. Somehow, perhaps it reminded me of my singleness.

Whatever my thought was about having a fling with this guy, I was taking it seriously.

But what is taking it seriously? I didn't take the appropriate action to discuss our future or put down any boundaries. I was afraid, afraid to move forward, to be rejected, to be alone, to be left with the pain of my loss. I was clinging. Hoping. Waiting my bloody time.

Flash forward a few more months, and he's getting jealous. I dance with some guy at a party, and he's not happy. He sees a message on my phone from an ex I've known for many years, a relationship that took place before we even got together, and my man is ready to leave. I beg him to stay and explain to him that I'm confused about the status of our relationship.

He never discusses his wife, or what he wants out of our relationship. In fact, he becomes very defensive when I try to inquire about it or tell him I want more. I leave and vow never to return. He gives. Little more, I go back, ad infinitum. It's the classic, toxic relationship.

In another conversation, he tells me if he had his own choice, he would still be married. That hurt like a punch in the face.

I broke up with him but couldn't keep my distance. That's because I didn't have enough power or faith to turn onwards for my sustenance.

I lacked power. This is why it's so crucial to have a higher power to lean on,

So, do not fear, for I am with you; do not be dismayed, for I am your God. I will strengthen you and help you; I will uphold you

Isaiah 41:10

I gave the lawyer my power, but in the end, the distress I struggled with led me to deepen my relationship with Jesus in a new and powerful way

he took up all my thinking and feeling space. He inhabited the spaces that were for me. I couldn't be with myself. The pain of my former relationship was too much to face, it felt that way.

I wanted so much to be chosen by him, I wanted him to make everything better, to make me feel loved and valuable - I had forgotten how to choose myself and give all those things I sought from my relationships to myself.

A man like this wouldn't chose ANYONE. He couldn't even choose himself. And this precisely why I pursued him because that's how powerful these love constellations are. Or should I say that's how powerfully the wounds within us are - for their gravitas constellates these very sophisticated defensive behaviours.

Don't settle for a relationship that won't let you be yourself

–Oprah Winfrey

They drive us to fulfil the limiting beliefs we hold about ourselves at all costs. They keep us in our relational comfort zone. Because we are afraid to believe and declare that we can have the love we want and deserve. Yes, ladies, we really can. But we have to show up so it honours what we want in a relationship. We have to not settle for less.

I know this relationship is awful, but I can't seem to stop. I am so disconnected from myself.

Girls you gotta know when it's time to turn the page

—Tori Amos

In my relationship with myself, I am doing exactly what he is doing to me; being unavailable to myself. Abandoning myself, just like he is abandoning me.

Whenever I attempt to deepen the intimacy between us, he becomes defensive and angry. Making excuses about his suffering and divorce. Look, if the man isn't giving you what you want in the moment, honestly? Walk.

But to love yourself takes time. I was getting stronger every day, and more conscious that this was not healthy. I would lie awake, heart pounding, fingers and toes throbbing, feeling like I'm dying or losing my mind, this compounded by the fact that my daughter was asleep in her room next door. I was so anxious.

I remember just staring at the empty pillow next to me, and it hit me. I said, "Nancy, where is he? Why isn't he here?

You've been in a relationship with him for over two years. Every week he would stick strictly to a schedule of twice a week when my daughter was at her father's.

Do not try to change people they are only messengers telling you who you are. Revalue yourself and they will confirm the change.

–Neville Goddard

He only lives 15 minutes down the road. Why are you going through all this anxiety alone? Night after night. Don't you think you deserve to be with someone who wants to commit to you? My internal dialogue was becoming more mature. I would find the street to walk away. But it took quite some time.

I obeyed the prompting of my inner wisdom, the courage that said, you deserve more; Do not fear what's within, you can face it, you have d=God to protect and strengthen you. Let him go, Nancy.

It was if I was sick - I mean like, hospital sick. Every night I got on my knees and prayed and cried and cried and prayed, and the most miraculous sequence of events conspired to teach me that a lack of self-love was my problem.

It seemed every song, overheard conversation, youtube video, or book I came across was another piece of information on my journey back to the deepest, truest authentic self.

I was spending time with me, writing, reconnecting, praying, becoming alive again, learning to honour me. I wrote this book during that period of my life. As painful as it was, something so wonderful came out of it.

As for me, I'm embracing all those things that have hurt me because I'm serious about getting the love I deserve.

I am also serious about knowing that every single man you attract is a mirror. That terrible man showed me how little I valued myself. We are not victims, and we waste time despising or blaming the men who have treated us badly. Leave them to God.

Focus on repairing what needs to be repaired in your self-esteem and self-love. Focus on creating a new conception of yourself, starting with the future self you imagine yourself to be, not a past traumatised self.

> *Much of the pain in broken relationships stems from the truth that many of us in western culture have never been serious students of love. We haven't really taken it seriously enough to learn how it actually works.*
>
> –The 5 Love languages
>
> Gary Chapman

Believe with every part of you you will have the husband or partner of your dreams, whatever that may look like for you. And never give up until he shows up, oh and set the table for two, because he's coming.

Do not run away from the emotional pain in your romantic relationships, USE IT as a roadmap to your dry places. Let your heartaches, losses and disappointments in love guide you to the richest, most abundant places in yourself. Allow your relationship struggles to show you what needs repair, attention and more love. Be creative, do a vision board, write poetry, draw. Just use your pain to create. Something wonderful is always borne out of pain.

Do this work. Don't settle for less, and you will attract the love most can only dream of girl.

Emotional pain cracks you open, through those cracks, God can breathe brightest, light, power and authenticity into your soul. This inhaling of God's breath into you, will cause such great expansion, beyond all you can think or imagine.

I have invested over 10 years helping people discover how to emotionally connect hit themselves to find love. Ho w to actively die and receive love instead of passively waiting for it to magically happen.

If you read and apply the information in this book you will discover how to give and receive love more effectively.

You will discover the missing ingredient in some of your past relationships, and you will learn how to build loving, exciting, safe and mutually supportive relationships; by learning your love constellation, you will naturally notice what actions constellates in your partner when they are feeling threatened too.

This week we have gained a much deeper understanding of ourselves emotionally. We have seen how our childhood experiences have set us up to create certain types of love experiences and we see how we can unravel ourselves from this.

> I said: What about my eyes?
>
> God said: Keep them on the road.
>
> I said; What about my passion?
>
> God said: Keep it burning
>
> I said; What about my heart?
>
> God Said; Tell me what you hold inside it.
>
> I said: Pain and Sorrow.

We see that with enough self-love, we have the power to create something different and release ourselves form our parents' legacy.

So, much hope is in the air, as we breathe in this reality; a truth that self-love really does have the potential to change our relationships, to change who, and what we attract, and even our whole wide world.

Reflection & Discussion Questions

1. How will you wake yourself from the trance of limiting beliefs the next time you feel yourself collapsing into one?

2. What thoughts did you have when doing the love constellation diagrams?

3. Who has your self-love journey been like?

4. Men as Mirrors. Think about one relationship where you can see the way your partner treated you is the exact way you were treating yourself. Discuss

5. Write about your most painful relationship. Create a poem, short story, vision board or painting to describe what was going on for you.

Step 3

SURRENDER

Reconnecting to Your Higher Power

This is where *surrender* really begins and you *decide* that there is something that can help you evolve beyond the painful patterns you learned in childhood.

Suppose you are serious about getting the love you want, and I know you are. In that case, it's time to become teachable, prepared to take direction from an external source, and decide to implement the power of prayer, self-reflection and meditation into your life.

It's time for us to give up self-reliance in favour of reliance on a higher power, whatever that may look like to you. (Remember, your concept of a higher power should make sense to you. (Never mind what anyone else is doing or thinks about you.)

We learn to practice humility and we strive to put character-building ahead of comfort daily. We purposefully practise honesty, tolerance, and true love of man and God as our daily basis of living.

We have now accepted that humility is necessary in achieving a sober and fulfilled life. Over time, with persistent practice of spiritual principles in all areas of our lives, we come to see that our perspective has evolved into a less self-centered life to a much more humble, selfless one.

Daily conscious contact with a God of your understanding will transform your relationship with yourself and others.

WeeK 3

This week, you will surrender to the wisdom and guidance of your higher power.

You will begin to implement new daily practices that will keep you connected to yourself and guide you towards deeper inner-child healing.

Daily conscious contact with yourself and your higher power is a major component of your romantic relationship recovery.

The tips, quotes and songs this week are aimed at reconnecting you to God for the purpose of healing and restoring belief in a future where relationships are everything you ever dreamed of.

You might find yourself enjoying more solitude this week. Take out your journal and keep notes of all you feel and think and try to remember and write down your dreams.

Now, take a deep breath, channel Tamela Mann, and repeat after me three times:

"God provides, so why do I worry about my life?

When you come to my rescue a thousand times

Every other voice it is a lie

God provides...

This is because when you are discomforted or in emotional pain you will look inwards for comfort and validation and not outwards to your partner—it is NOT your partner's job to straighten out your unresolved emotional struggles, at least not in the first instance.

Learning how to heal your childhood traumas, self-soothe, and be less reactive in your relationships is a journey you must travel alone in the first instance,

Your partner can support you along the way, but this is an inside job. One between you and your God as you walk a spiritual path toward greater wholeness.

So, what is the science behind prayer? We know that prayer and meditation are powerful because they focus our thoughts on something outside ourselves.

Research backs the idea that meditation and prayer can trigger the release of feel-good chemicals in the brain. So, look, you can't lose.

Tip:

Dr. Loretta G. Breuning, founder of the Inner Mammal Institute and author of *The Science of Positivity* and *Habits of a Happy Brain*, explains that when we pray, we can activate neural pathways we developed when young to release hormones such as oxytocin.

"Scientists are making the first attempts to understand spiritual experience–and what happens in the brains and bodies of people who believe they connect with the divine.

The field is called 'neurotheology,' and although it is new, it's drawing prominent researchers in the U.S. and Canada. Scientists have found that the brains of people who spend untold hours in prayer and meditation are different."

– Barbera Bradley Hagerty

"Oxytocin is known for its role in maternal labor and lactation, but it also [enables] **social trust and attachment, giving us a good feeling despite living in a world of threat,**" says Dr. Breuning.

She goes on to say, "It's the idea of, 'I can count on something to protect me.' When a situation comes up and you're out of ideas and you are helpless, feeling much like you did when you were a baby, prayer can provide some other source of hope."

So, we turn to a higher intelligence for guidance. And we get to have hope, to heal our relationships with ourselves and our relationship with the *threatening* world around us, which is not threatening at all, unless we perceive it to be.

Now, take a deep breath, channel Michael Buble and repeat after me:

When you're smilin', when you're smilin'

The whole world smiles with you

When you're laughin', when you're laughin'

The sun comes shinin' through

But when you're cryin', you bring on the rain

So, stop your sighin', be happy again

Keep on smilin', 'cause when you're smilin'

The whole world smiles with you.

Remembering that your best reasoning got you not so far in love, it's time to surrender your relationship struggles to a God of your understanding, to the power of prayer, mindfulness and self-reflection.

Seek professional help if guided to do so and trust that the guidance in this book will help with your relationship recovery.

Accepting and following the guidance of God and believing He will transform your life gives us the power to let go of our old limiting beliefs; with a new higher intelligence governing us, we can release the childhood story that we aren't worthy of love and that we have to work hard to be worthy of love— the powerlessness this story has created in our lives is indescribable. Today, we decide to turn our will and our lives over to a God of our understanding and to implement all the actions of prayer, meditation and faith into our lives.

To let go of this old story, we will need discipline and have at the back of our minds that our best thinking and greatest intentions got us nowhere in our quest to find lasting love.

We dated or married men when we were not ready for mature love. We ignored our inner voice, knowing that something inside of us wasn't right. We drank too much, overfed, worked too hard, tried too hard, and allowed our self-will to run riot. It's time to make a decision that will serve us and stick to those decisions. But we will need the help of a higher power if we hope to make this transition.

We projected untruths onto the men we dated, accusing them of being selfish, emotional illiterate or unworthy on some way - because we needed to turn them into people who would disappoint us; after all, that's what we were used to in our childhood relationships and unless we break the spell our childhood *still* has over us in adulthood we are destined to keep creating painful dynamics in love.

So, we distorted things to fit our old story and we sabotaged our relationships out of fear. Fear we weren't good enough and didn't deserve love. We had no idea that all this conflict was going on inside of us all the while. We just thought we were unlucky in love. We couldn't understand why he wouldn't just love us. We may have even convinced ourselves that we didn't want a serious relationship anyway.

The truth is we are blessed beyond belief.

This week, we will come to terms with one simple truth. Without our higher power and the discipline of deciding and sticking to them, we have no chance of overcoming our old story permanently. It is too powerful and too entrenched within us. We will need to buckle down this week.

And so, we become willing to do what it takes to put God first in our lives. We know that when we put God first, we put ourselves first. We set our intention towards a lifelong relationship with our higher power, who will show us how valuable we are and how to love ourselves.

We anticipate the stormy waters ahead because we know change isn't easy; we tried a million ways to wrestle with our problems with men, hoping to change them or make things better, but in the end, we could change nothing. Still, we stayed even though we left once and vowed never to return to him, knowing he wasn't meeting our needs.

Many of us have difficulty with closure and letting go. We seek closeness from those who are avoidant and unavailable—gravitating towards a familiar pattern from childhood.

Many of us have never known how to love ourselves; we learned at a very young age how to put another's needs before our own, and so when that type of dynamic shows up, when someone in a relationship requires us to abandon ourselves, we oblige and proceed to we cling on to it, as we did to the unavailable and abandoning parent that we needed back then.

We are adults left holding on to this old story, like a bunch of rotten cabbages that are stinking up our lives. We're desperate to let it go, yet we don't know how to let it go since it doesn't serve us.

We only know we have outgrown the old behaviours of being afraid that love will hurt us. Tired of loving too much to avoid rejection or giving away our power to hang on to him, or trying so hard to keep his love, not speaking up and honouring what we truly feel. We viewed things through a distorted prism of not being enough or not deserving love. Enough is enough.

And so, we hand it all over with this prayer.

> "[Praying in part] is saying to myself: I am really hurting about X. I am really hoping for Y. I am looking for support from Z, as a repeated practice, prayer can serve as a useful habit for times when we're overwhelmed or struggling to figure out a solution."
>
> – Dr. Loretta G. Breuning, founder of the Inner Mammal Institute and author of The Science of Positivity and Habits of a Happy Brain.

Step 3 Prayer:

God, I offer myself to Thee to

build with me and to do with me as Thou wilt.

Relieve me of the bondage of self,

that I may better do Thy will.

Take away my difficulties,

that victory over them may bear witness to those I would help

of Thy Power, Thy Love, and Thy Way of life.

May I do Thy will always!

Now, for crying out loud, please don't panic. Remember, offering yourself and your will to your higher power is simply offering yourself to YOUR highest self.

That highest self part of you always whispers to be careful or love yourself more. That part of you that tells you, "You can do anything," or "You are worth so much more than you are accepting."

That still small voice has always been there for you, which has never abandoned you. Even when you had your dark night of the soul, *something was there with you,* gently comforting you, softly pulling you away from looking outside for answers, gently prompting you to seek within. Always encouraging you to put yourself first and pay attention to your inner knowing—that is God.

You can never go wrong deciding to completely surrender to this power, for the power is you. It is the highest and best version of yourself.

You are not giving yourself over to some distant deity to rule over you and dominate your will. Oh no, God is Source, the power that creates worlds and that created you. God is the best *you* can ever be.

Decide to put yourself first, starting with the energy that creates worlds and starting now. And feel an inner peace and confidence you have never ever felt before. When we surrender to God, the first thing that happens is that we begin to receive guidance about which areas of our lives need more peace and healing. Usually, we will be directed to places that are hurting within us. Our inner child.

Releasing Drama and Inner-Child Healing

The way we release the drama and heal our inner child is to shift from our traumatised centre to our adult power centre. We must initiate an ongoing mentoring relationship with our inner child to do this. This is what I call "The crossover."

It is made possible by synthesising the little girl part of you that is still holding on to the hurts and ideas that she is not worthy or not enough with the empowered, strong adult part of you into a dynamic-interdependent tapestry. Imagine it like an inner relational eco system that sustains, nourishes, and feeds itself. It's a beautiful thing.

Once you enter the new relationship with yourself, you will no longer experience dramatic shifts in yourself, shifts that show up in a dissociative way. One minute you can be empowered, the next, something triggers you and you feel very small and worthless. These states will move into more congruency and fluidity, a deeper sense of oneness with self, as you allow, accept and soothe all the parts of yourself into one flowing, healthy system of self-relating. This is true self-love.

It can be quite disturbing this feeling of being split into two. I remember often seeing my boyfriends staring at me in bewilderment saying, "But what's wrong with you? Why are you acting like this? You were fine just yesterday? Or "But nothing's changed, why are you upset now?"

I could be triggered in a breath by something he did or I saw on TV or a song. Anything could shift me from my adult centre and I would collapse into my afraid and desperate, insecure and anxious child self, who is now petrified that she will lose her man's love or be rejected.

> "By staying open-minded and listening to the needs and desires of your inner child, you open yourself up to the possibilities of anything..."
>
> -Kim Ha Campbell.

When triggered in this way, I move swiftly into survival mode and begin either, seeking safety from my partner, or withdrawing altogether. Either way, I am seeking a realigning that can only come from getting still, and lovingly mentoring my traumatised child self back into peace and alignment. You dig?

Cultivating this mentoring relationship between these adult and child parts of oneself is a critical tool for any woman who is serious about releasing the split inside of her and the blame and expectations and the toxicity she brings to her relationships.

For it is the young part of herself that creates the toxic dynamics in her relationships.

Your adult self will mentor your child self. This new dynamic synthesis will mean that YOU are the one loving the man you choose. Not the little girl inside of you. With your adult self running things in your relationship, you can offer your partner consistency, peace, understanding, and space.

It is NOT your partner's job to take care of the little girl in you. The **adult, you must take care of the child part in you,** giving her all the love and compassion she needs, nursing her out of fear and back to health and balance, allowing her to express her voice and feelings. When you feel a deep sadness or are triggered, you go and spend time with the younger part of yourself—ask her:

1. Sweetheart, how are you feeling?

2. What do you need?

3. What is your memory right now?

4. How is what you are feeling or remembering affecting you?

Find more of your own questions, ask her about specific events if they come up for you. Really listen. Imagine your little girl is sitting in your lap in front of you. Connect with her. Comfort her. Make her safe again. This is how you mentor your inner child.

As with any mother-daughter relationship, there must be boundaries, boundaries make children feel safe. Your adult self, who is healthy, strong and emotionally literate, remains in charge. The adult part of you is charged with guiding and protecting the child, who has no idea how to create health and safety in her relationships.

Your inner child does not get to dictate your moods, feelings or choices, she does not get to drive your relationships. Not anymore.

This new inner relationship will not only deepen the self-love you have with yourself but will also bring about deeper integration and wholeness. This will revolutionise the way you love, offering you new and deeper ways to love. Without all the anxiety and fear you used to feel in your relationships.

Making this mentoring exercise a part of your everyday life will give you independence, a lightness, a sense that you can make decisions and love freely without the heaviness of a wounded and uncontained child within—ever threatening to pop up and disrupt your peace at any given moment.

Now, close your eyes, and take a deep inhale. It is time to get the inner peace and loving, reciprocal, calm relationship you deserve. With yourself!

Now, take a deep breath, channel Donna Summer and repeat after me three times:

Ooh I feel love, I feel love

I feel love, I feel love

I feel love

I feel love

I feel love

This Is What Self-Love Looks Like

So, this is what self-love looks like in practice. Working with all your parts to create a rich and dynamic inner life, where trauma and pain are managed by a stronger, capable, loving you.

As you work through these steps with me, this is taking place within you. We have acquired a new merger; now, all you need is to invite our higher power to the party and we're all set. We're doing some serious business!

A new nexus is being formed within the emotional core of your body. From this new centre within, all the love you have ever sought from men as well as the love you didn't receive as a child will fill you from within, pour into you.

You will feel a new sense of wholeness, rootedness and self-love. And you will open up new choice points for yourself. You begin to bust out of what author and psychotherapist Katherine Woodward Thomas refers to as your "prisonality."

We must find micro-processes to shift from the traumatised centre to the powerful adult centre. Whichever centre we are in, we will generate our lives from that place and if we generate our lives from the traumatised centre we will create evidence that the hurt little girl inside of us and her disempowered beliefs about relationships are true. They are NOT true.

> Don't Break Your Own Heart:
> "Self-love seems so often unrequited."
>
> – Anthony Powell

The little girl inside of us who may have suffered from a less than perfect childhood is still holding on to those hurts. She still believes she is unlovable, unworthy, a burden, disposable, replaceable and any other messages she may have picked up.

The remedy to this is to always keep the adult you at the helm of your ship, or at the centre of yourself, reassuring you, listening, being attentive to your feelings. Comforting yourself, writing in your journal, getting still. The adult self is vigilant about being there for the child within. This paying attention to your feelings, being attentive to what your inner child is communicating to you, becomes your norm, a part of your everyday life and interactions.

You need to develop a mentoring relationship with the strong, capable adult you and the little girl within still holding on to old hurts for this to work.

It's about creating a relationship with the little girl part of you by acknowledging, validating and being attentive whenever some life situation triggers this part of you. Remember, we all experience times in our relationships when we feel empowered and healthy. We must be alert for any trigger that drives us to collapse back into the trauma centre, to the hurt little girl inside of us.

The hurt little girl in us encourages us to self-abandon, prioritize others over self, ignore our inner knowing, lack courage and confidence, and become desperate and needy, fumbling about on our decisions. The little girl within is unsteady and seeks fulfilment at all costs, we NEVER let our little girl date or lead our relationships. EVER.

Your inner child does not want to lead your relationships anyway. She only disrupts things in your relationships when triggered. This is because she wants you to see and comfort her when she feels fear, insecure or anxiety, just like a 4-year-old acts up when she's afraid. Your inner child is no different. She is always there waiting for YOU to love her. Do not put her up for adoption for others to take care of her. She is YOUR responsibility to nurture and make safe whenever she comes up in you because if she is not mentored, she can become a dangerous lion devouring your power and destabilising your love life. Don't say I didn't warn ya!

The tools to keep this lion/child trauma part of ourselves calm and resting safely within us have arrived.

Good question. Why have we had to suffer so long? It took me until my 40s to begin to shift any of this stuff and evolved beyond the insecure attachment styles and codependent patterns in my relationships. They are difficult to modify.

Well, it's simple. We could not shift our toxic pattern because we try to do it at the level of our intellect. We go to therapy or read books to try to "figure shit out," but the truth is the BODY holds the power. All your old hurts and traumas are held in the body, around where the abdomen is.

Our childhood trauma and all the big uncontrollable feelings we have are held in our bodies! So, our inquiries and conclusions start at the wrong level of analysis.

This is why after years of therapy we are still not changing. We are not meeting the problem where it is.

The problem is in the traumatised child self. And that self is centred in your body somatically. Not in the mind. To analyse, we need perspective, and perspective requires distance. But inner-child healing calls for connection, not distance.

So, we go to therapy or coaching and have some success and breakthroughs on a cognitive level, but we are still holding the trauma on a somatic level. It is stuck there in your abdomen.

But we are not accustomed to turning inwards for replenishment, love, security and wholeness. We are culturally conditioned towards looking outside of ourselves for sustenance. Ladies, we got some changing to do, but don't sweat it, take a deep breath, channel the Dixie Chicks and repeat after me:

Well, I've been afraid of changin'

'Cause I've built my life around you

But time makes you bolder

Even children get older

And I'm getting older too

You have been afraid of changing because you've been so attached to and led by the traumatised part of you. You've built much of your life around loving men, and abandoning yourself while doing so. This was in the hope that they could fill the powerful void you have within, that they could make you feel safe. You have never felt safe because you do not foundational sense of safety nor do you have a way to access safety within you. Not until now. The education in this book is grating a new foundation from which you can build. Don't worry about it, I got you, babe,

You have allowed the traumatised child part of you to do the loving, to make the choices and to lead you. But now you have a deeper understanding of what has occurred within. This changes everything.

All this inner chaos has made it impossible to be a woman who can attract a stable, honest, communicative, emotionally healthy man. If you can learn to trust your higher power and draw upon your spiritual resources to know she is loved unconditionally and that every decision she makes will always lead her to her treasure. So, this is what self-love looks like in practice—working with all the parts of you towards one whole self. Create a rich and dynamic inner life where trauma and pain are managed by a stronger, capable, loving you.

Place your hand on your abdomen now and become conscious that your pain is residing in there. Little dense consolidations of old hurts need to be dissolved. Otherwise, we will always be reactive in our relationships.

We engage in embodiment practices such as deep breathing and deep envisaging. Phillip Shepherd, author of *Radical Wholeness* and leader in the Global Embodiment Movement, said to me when I asked him about love and losing oneself in relationships, "We will never lose ourselves in love if we have found ourselves in the body."

By being embodied, we are conscious of what is happening within us. Your adult self must tend to the traumatised child self by speaking directly to her. By mentoring and loving her. The way to heal from codependency is to develop a mentoring relationship with the two parts of you, the child and the adult hurting child part of you, with love and leadership.

This will rearrange your internal structure and so all romantic experiences will be processed through the adult you. But it is hard to learn a new way of relating to self; it's scary to let go of being led and take charge of yourself, but it's okay. We're not getting any younger and if we want that powerful love we deserve, changes need to be made. Don't sweat it.

Now take a deep breath and channel those Dixie Chicks again and repeat after me:

Well, I've been afraid of changin'

'Cause I've built my life around you

But time makes you bolder

Even children get older

And I'm getting older too

The little girl in us allowed us to be used, mistreated, abandoned, lied to, misled, and deceived, such was her low self-worth and desperation to be loved. When we can generate feelings of love, safety, joy, inspiration from writing, we are winning in love. Because we did not love ourselves and because we sought healing and love from men rather than God. We manipulated, abused, controlled and hurt the men in our lives to make them validate us.

Men have no idea how to heal or fix us, it's not their job, and they are busy trying to improve themselves from their difficult childhoods.

Remember, every man you ever had a relationship with was your mirror, mirroring the relationship you were having with yourself. They were treating you the way you treated yourself. So, it's highly probable they didn't love themselves either; it's an all-round mirroring process.

Name: Phillip Sheldon

Location; London

Humiliation Factor 10/10

Phillip, Ah yes, he was charming and funny, and we had chemistry. I thought he would be the perfect person to complete my life and make me happy—rich, handsome and successful, of course, that was my conscious thought. My unc onscious and deepest thought was that this trifling player would never be enough to take seriously. This, he was the perfect choice. Let the games begin!

> *The purpose of a relationship is not to have another who might complete you, but to have another who might share your completeness*
>
> *-Neale Donald wasch*

I found out he was cheating on me by looking through his phone and seeing a naked woman's picture. He denied it all, but not so long after that. I decided to pay him an early morning visit. At this stage, we had been dating for a year.

I sat outside in the taxi, peering up at his fifth-floor window of his swanky glass building in Knightsbridge. *Why is his TV on at 2:00 a.m.?* I asked myself. When I spoke to him at about 9:00 p.m. that evening, he had said he was going "straight" to bed? This motherfucker was trifling, I thought. So, was the highly amused and giggling taxi man that drove me there. Embarrassing.

Upon seeing the TV light, I knew something was not right. I dashed across the large road and entered his building, heart-pounding, ready for anything. I knew the porter was his little watchdog, so I just barged past his porter and hurled myself into the lift, prodding the buttons furiously until the door closed just in time before the porter was able to stop me. You know those ones when you're ready, ladies, ratings off, whatever!

It was a disaster; he had someone in there and refused to open the door. I was so desperate. I called the police and told them he had my expensive jewellery and was refusing to give it back. This was a lie; I just wanted them to open the door to see what I already knew—that there was another woman in there. Part of me also wanted to catch him, to reinforce my story that I would always be disappointed in my relationships; that I would always be the girl who is never chosen.

I still went back with him after that and believed his lies. Such was the magnitude of my lack of self-love. It wasn't long before I caught him cheating again, but here's the big bit: When we do not love ourselves, we can't love anyone else; have you heard that before?

I ignored my instincts and instead spent all my time and energy thinking about Hussein, trying to please him, catch him, or make him love me.

All the while, I was waiting for me to pay attention to myself and the things I was feeling inside. My priority should have been myself, but I would 'open the door to me! Instead, I cheated on myself, put someone else before me and left me out in the cold. No surprise why Hussein treated me in the exact same way that I was already treating myself! That's what I mean, when I say relationships are mirroring the relationship we are having with ourselves. Can you see where this is going?

Do you know what it means? Here's what it means. I didn't love myself and I didn't love Phillip , and deep down I didn't care that he was cheating; otherwise, I would have walked when I saw his TV on at 2:00 a.m. and ran upstairs to find he wouldn't open the door to me.

But I didn't walk because I wanted something from him and it wasn't love. I wanted anything to stop my pain, my emptiness, my sense that deep down, I was unworthy of healthy, lasting love. I was just like an addict. Deep down, an addict couldn't care less about the welfare of his dealer or what kind of person he is; he just wants to score so he can fill the void within him.

And so, when we are codependent or self-abandoning, we are not *actually* doing it for love, we are not even in love with these men; what we are doing with them is trying to get something that is missing inside of us filled up.

We are selfish in our relationships and self-centered. We need our fix and we don't mind hurting ourselves or anyone else to get it.

We want to get out of the relationship what we need, and we don't know how to care that much about the person we're involved with because our needs are so enormous that the other person gets absorbed by them. Whether we are super needy or massively withdrawn and holding back, it's the same thing. We are trying to fill a void and anyone who gets in our way is collateral damage.

> "Relationship is more than the cohabiting together to provide you with the means to survive and procreate; it is actually a journey into finding the deep truth of who you are."
>
> Anonymous

Maybe that's why we attracted such emotionally bereft men because we were just like them. But all that's about to change.

In this step, we allow a higher power to take over our thinking and our actions so that we can learn how to attract a king of a man who will treat us like the queen that we never fully understood we were until now.

Now, take a deep breath, channel TLC, and repeat after me.

I don't want no scrubs;

a scrub is a guy who can't get no love from me!

When we don't love ourselves, we will inevitably attract *the wrong* type of partner, why? Because self-love puts you on a healing journey to discover what things in your past are holding you back. No person goes unscathed in life. Whatever dysfunctions occurred in the households of your childhood and adolescent years affected you.

Your partner will enact aspects that "trigger" the unhealed or unresolved parts of you, which brings them to the forefront. This is because romantic relationships invite you to heal the childhood attachment and developmental wounds that keep you from wholeness.

You can no longer hide or keep hidden the sacred wounds of the past. They pop up whenever there is a similarity between something in the present and something that was hurtful from the past. Something like a loved one's absence, closeness to another, or needing space.

Self-love is not a destination, it is a process and it takes a lifetime. Guys like Phillip are a fine a dozen, but they are also blessings, they give us the coordinates to find our way back home to ourselves, so don't be so quick to judge yourself, and if you're stuck in a bad romance, let it teach you all you need to know about how to love you.

Because we have confidence and inner strength now, a high power that resides within us filing us with faith and directing our thinking, we are no longer fragile and needy. We are self-directing, self-possessed, full of confidence and taking charge of ourselves in relationships. By reading this book, you are acquiring the tools to generate self-love and feelings of worth and safety from within.

The other better news is that we are not alone for the first time, perhaps ever in our lives. We have a God on whom we can depend, who will strengthen us and teach us how to love ourselves unconditionally. From here onwards, we simply cannot go wrong.

When we live our lives with an awareness that our attention must be turned inwards to find love and validation – towards ourselves and the God within – we no longer look outside of ourselves to our relationships for validation. Instead, we seek wisdom and guidance from ourselves.

If we don't straighten and practice this inwardly for comfort and guidance, we will unavoidably give our power to the guys we become involved with. Without a higher power, we are like ships sailing on stormy waters with no sails to direct us. We are just swayed about by currents of lust, emptiness, fear, neediness and codependency, leading us to a destination we did not choose.

When I took Step Three for the first time, my problems with alcohol and cocaine disappeared instantly. The fact that I was part of a fellowship and had regular interaction. With what was my tribe at the time was invaluable. That's why I encourage you to sign up to my Facebook group and become part of a sisterhood, where we support each other, make great friends and enjoy our journey together. Learning to have a life and love we could only dream of before.

> *"Not only do prayer and spiritual practice reduce stress, but just twelve minutes of meditation per day may slow down the aging process.*
>
> *Contemplating a loving God rather than a punitive God reduces anxiety and depression and increases feelings of security, compassion, and love.*
>
> *Intense prayer and meditation permanently change numerous structures and functions in the brain, altering your values and the way you perceive reality."*
>
> *-From the book How God Changes Your Brain by Andrew Newberg & Mark Robert Waldman*

I never indulged daily in the first place, mainly at weekends, but I used alcohol and drugs to cope with my unconscious feelings of low self-worth. I do drink today, but I do not smoke or use any drugs. I had a full 11 years of complete sobriety. Just what I needed to begin the healing journey back to myself.

I used alcohol to cope with my emptiness and resentments and the things I could never forgive others or myself for. Step Three isn't some miracle thing in and of itself, it is the act behind it that contains the miracle.

Step Three means taking *action* to turn to a higher power for guidance, and I did that, by implementing daily practices into my life that slowed me down and helped me to become more disciplined, peaceful and ego-driven. With God, your life is not fear-based; it is faith-based and less carnal. With this type of foundation, you can have anything and everything you've ever wanted.

I know it sounds miraculous, that's because it is. Step Three is magical. Suddenly, I found it easy to resist. I had power for the first time in my life; I had control over myself and discipline to make good decisions for me. Ultimately, without faith, recovering your power to change your life remains out of reach. Actively believing in and embracing a higher power is an act of both surrender and courage. A new self-love and power will take over your life.

I retake this step sometimes daily, sometimes hourly, sometimes minute by minute. Surrendering to a higher power is a commitment that can be remade as often as you need to. Some days, we are pulled back into old thinking and habits or plagued with fear. During these times we recommit to total surrender to God. We reinstate His place in the driving seat of our lives and allow a higher intelligence to restore our minds and hearts to balance and health.

Your higher power is indwelling within you, giving you strength and teaching you how to give your all to yourself. To be the one you can always depend on. The more you rely on God the more you will have the power to love yourself and put yourself first.

Turn inwards and seek conscious contact with the God of your understanding who is your special place. The one place you turn to repeatedly to replenish and fill up on positive energy and self-belief.

Every day I turn to the God of my understanding in one way or another. I get on my knees and pray for guidance and the willingness to change. I pray for wisdom and acceptance. You might be familiar with this prayer. It's the Step Three prayer. You can use it every day, morning and night, or you can just talk to God about whatever you want to talk about. It's up to you to be sure to have conscious contact with the God of your understanding every day.

If You Like It Then You Gotta Put a Ring on It

So, ladies, in a nutshell, this is where you put a ring on it. Yes, you put a ring on your OWN finger. You make a commitment to love yourself first and foremost, to make yourself the priority, forsaking all others, till death and you still don't even part.

When you connect to a higher power, you have a sustainable self-servicing relationship with yourself. You have everything you need right there within you. Now, take a deep breath, channel Chris Brown and repeat after me three times:

You got it, girl, you got it (ayy)

You got it, girl, you got it

Flaws and all, I love 'em all, to me, you're perfect

Baby girl, you got it, girl, you got it, girl (oh-oh)

You got it, girl, you got it, girl (ooh)

My whole life, I've waited for someone to come into my life and change it. Before really learning how to love and take care of myself, I thought this only happened in a relationship. I waited for someone who could make me happy and secure, love me and never leave me like my mother did when she died of cancer when I was only 17.

That was 30 years ago, and it took me a long time to see that the only person who can honestly give me the love and security I was seeking is me. I am hoping I can save you a bit of time here.

> "To love oneself is the beginning of a lifelong romance."
>
> Oscar wilde

I know it might sound a bit corny, but you are the one that you have been waiting for. No one can ever love you unconditionally like you can. No one can give you their undivided attention, time, loyalty, truth, and communication like you can.

So, that's what I mean when I say it's time to put a ring on it. You may have some painful feelings about yourself, some feelings of low self-worth.

That might be why you've always waited for someone else to love and validate you. I know because that's how it was for me. But you are your soul mate, the only one who can properly love you.

Step Three is the step that directs you towards your higher power to learn how to feel whole and worthy. It means that before this higher intelligence can help you, you have to have faith. Faith that God is real and that He will love you, comfort you and guide you in a way you have never experienced before.

Faith is, without a doubt, required and the Bible confirms this by saying, "Faith without works is dead." We can have faith yet keep God out of our lives. I have always had a relationship with God. I would often pray to Him and get angry when my relationships were not working. I would pray to Him to 'give' me certain men I wanted to marry or be committed to, only to discover years later that had my prayers been answered, it would have been a total catastrophe.

My self-will was so strong. I wanted them, so I prayed for God to give them to me, these were some of the worst decisions I could ever have made and I thank God He didn't answer the prayers.

In those instances, I had not decided to turn my will and life over to God. Instead, I decided to get God to submit to my will. It didn't work. Fear, lust, arrogance, entitlement are just some of the character defects that push God out of our lives. Please do not be deceived.

Deciding to turn your will and lives over to God's care as we understand it means genuinely doing that. No half measures. Commit to this like you wanted to commit to that man you loved, remember him? Begin listening to your inner knowing; slow down, spend time in silence, cultivate a relationship with the God within you. Just take the first step and watch as it all unfolds.

Looking Back, It All Makes Sense

I know it hurts when you think back to all you have endured in the name of love. Maybe he betrayed you, lied consistently, or misled you, purposely not volunteering important information in some cruel game of hide and seek.

Was he deceitful, cruel, abusive, narcissistic, or just flat out indifferent? Was he avoidant, emotionally unavailable, or disconnected, always expecting you to open your life to him while he shut you out of his? Perhaps he was manipulative, never prepared to take responsibility, instead twisting the truth and making everything your fault.

Whatever your experience was with him, do you find your heart hurting some lonely nights and repeatedly asking yourself this simple question: "Why didn't he love me?" I know I asked myself this question many times. I sometimes still do.

Now, channel Beyonce, take a deep breath, and repeat after me three times:

Why don't you love me? (love me?)

Tell me, baby, why don't you love me (why don't you)

(Love me) When I make me so damn easy to love? (easy to love)

Why don't you need me?

Tell me, baby, why don't you need me

When I make me so damn easy to need? (oh-uh-oh-uuuuh)

> "Be yourself. No matter what others think God made you the way you are for a reason. Besides, an original is always more than a copy."
>
> Anonymous

But who is this question aimed at? Is it aimed at the man du jour, the husband? In my case, that question ran deep - the real pain I felt was that my Dad didn't love me.

When at its most reduced, the deep hurt of our past - the feeling of being unloved in our family of origin, will always superimpose itself onto our current adult relationships. That is, until we do the work to break the spell and bring it all into our consciousness.

Another question then, do we make it easy to love us? Do we really? How does the sense that we are not enough, carried over from childhood block us from being easy to love? We may try too hard, be constantly insecure, jealous, avoidant, cold, angry, blaming, any number of negative behaviours will spring from an insecure and wounded heart,

I remember with one guy I would sleep with my wig on every time he'd stay over, enduring the uncomfortable itching and sweating. Of course, it was unbearable, yet still, I dared not take it off; I could tell he preferred me with it on and, worst even, my hair underneath was beautiful.

I just wanted to be everything he wanted me to be. Now, is that making it easy to be loved? Not showing up authentically makes it impossible for the other person to get to know you, and if he's looking for a trophy, well, you'll do yourself a favour not playing up to that. He'll soon walk away, and that is no loss.

I'd wake at night to touch up my makeup or never remove my shape wear when he was around; I would wash like 10 times after being intimate with him as if trying to scrub myself out of the moment. As if I could wash myself into being someone else. Someone he wanted. And why did I do all of this? Because I didn't feel I was good enough as I was.

He could not love Nancy as she was and didn't understand that he wasn't worth giving my time to if he didn't love me as I was.

How could any of my partners love me when, one way or another, I never really let them see me? I wasn't present in my relationships. Instead, I was preoccupied with trying to hide—all the time. Hiding the real me to become the woman I thought they wanted. It was a maladaptive attempt to get love. A bad strategy, which left me more disconnected from me.

I guess I learned that putting another's needs before my own and abandoning myself and my needs got me love. But that was a long time ago. No victims. I'm not a child anymore.

Some days, I look back at how far I've come. I'm miles away from the girl who didn't love herself or the men in her life. Today it's so different. I can show up without my wig or shape wear or makeup. Because I insist on loving me and today, I know I'm enough most of the time. Besides, I'm attracting men who'd have it no other way.

Some days when I'm feeling a little insecure it's harder. My default setting is to hide myself and become what I think the other person wants to see. Still, we remember progress not perfection. I learned from a very young age that who I was wasn't enough, old patterns die hard. But we show up and keep on moving towards full self-love and acceptance. Towards greater wholeness.

So, now I'm dating. I can get a little impatient but I know when I feel lonely or any urgency it is usually because I'm disconnected from myself. I know what to do—pray, journal, lean into my purpose. Sing, laugh, hang out with friends, exercise, whatever it takes to get back into that self-love, feel-good vibration.

Because any man I attract will mirror my vibration and I don't want no unhappy, lacking brother stepping into my space. And so, I can wait for as long as it takes to see if he is right for me. I have not gotten physically intimate, which gives me time and space to get to know him and let him get to know me with no distractions.

> "A man {person} cannot be comfortable without his own approval."
>
> Mark Twain

When he is not available, it is easy to give him space without feeling rejected because I've got a life of my own that I love and, if I feel unsteady, a higher power that reminds me how worthy I am.

I've got a life that I've learned to love. When we are in a state of mind to put men before ourselves, we don't just reject ourselves and deny our lives and dreams. We reject the woman we know we can become, the powerful woman we know is inside of us.

I apologise to myself for mistreating my life and dismissing it so powerfully anytime a man came along. As if it was nothing, as if I was nothing. I give myself a big hug every time I think of it. Here is a poem about abandoning myself that I wrote about 25 years ago.

I'm doing okay, in my rather chic world, with my funny old life,

and my mixed up little head.

Writing poems, eating ice cream, burning incense, watching movies.

Lavender sachets in clothes drawers, swinging open new doors, I inhale the warm summer breeze...

I listen to my breath, in my solitary happiness, just basking in my very own peace.

And then, like a child who knows Santa's inside and placing presents under the tree, I hear your footsteps, feel an instant unrest, and my little heart's suddenly hungry. I leap from my chair, rush down the stairs, ice cream stains on my blouse.

At last, I'm saved, dragged back to a past where I'd follow my love to his 'house'. And just like that, my independence dispatched, I'm packed up and ready to leave home.

To swim in your seas, for you to rescue me because I've forgotten I am no longer drowning. A moment of regression, when you display some affection, and the 'horns' of old needs begin sounding.

It has been the case, not so long ago, when my home was an unfortunate place.

It was then that I began to seek within a man an idealistic and all-consuming solace. But that is no longer, for I am now stronger, able these days to generate my comfort.

And when I fall short, some people are sought, whose provision of care is more appropriate. Much like Dorothy, I've taken the journey only to realise everything I need is at my gate. And the needs I have inside, not the woman's but the child's, must not be served on my lover's plate.

It is not for my man to hold my child's hand and endure and labour to understand. The woman in me is who my lover will see, for she can let him be a real man.

I return to my chair, and blankly I stare as I recall my behaviour at its worst.

Sharing tears and much wisdom, from those who've lived some, the domino effect happens in reverse. My world begins to rebuild; my poems start to reveal and make sense of the things I need to work on.

> "The use of poetry continues to grow as a recognised form of therapy. More and more psychotherapists across the US, UK and Europe continue to use poetry therapy as part of their practice."
>
> Book Therapy

Then I fondly think of you and all that you do and I smile with a noble intention. And I thank all the lovers I've wanted as mothers who never were meant to be such. I am no longer Dorothy, with her good and bad wizardry, her confusion and misguided lusts.

I will not seek his salvation, nor his validation; in a relationship one and one means two

And I've made a discovery; my lover is not my cavalry, and my feet do not fit in his shoes.

With a foundation of my own, I can let his heart roam while I eat ice cream, watch movies, and do me.

I have wandered and roamed, looking for his love to make me a home that could live inside of me.

I finally realise real love is already inside and there's no place I'd rather be.

—Nancy Elliott (No Place Like Home) 2000

Poetry Challenge:

Why not try to write a poem of your own? Poetry is so healing. And the constraints of the rhymes, cadences and structure bring out the best in you. Give it a go; see if you can write a few lines about your patterns in relationships, this could be very cleansing for you.

New Beginnings

I challenge you today to take action. Prayer and faith are the fuel that lights the fire of action. Prayer and meditation are powerful tools for sure, but you also need to get out there and make changes. Invest in yourself; get help from professionals for your unresolved issues. Take a new course or class, figure out what lights your fire and don't wait around for a relationship to make you happy.

With love, release all the men you have loved with thanksgiving, knowing they have been God's little helpers along the way. Remember, your feelings of low self-worth, self-abandoning, lack of courage, lack of discipline and lacking any real power to make good designs for your life has its roots in your childhood; so, these traits existed in you long before you ever had your first romantic relationship or before meeting any of these men.

"The trick to balancing prayer with results is to recognize when is the time to pray/meditate and when is the time to go out and do something," says Hokemeyer. 'One of the purposes of prayer and meditation is to regain our footing so that we can step out into the world and take positive action: we reconnect, re-center, recharge and gain the strength necessary to take steps that will create real change. In other words, prayer is the fuel that lights the fire of action."

So, even if some of them were real dickey birds (and I'm sure some of them were), it's not their fault. You attracted them to can heal the dormant issues within you. That's how God works, He gives you the external circumstance to bring up and heal the inner problem. It's up to you to take the action and make the necessary changes to have that life and relationship you dream of.

As painful as it was, you needed these experiences to be where you are today. Don't worry about it. God knows what He is doing. Trust Him. And don't be offended that I refer to God as Him, it's just my language. You can find your own. Please don't let the way I do or say things put you off. Your old narrative is keen to drag you back to fear and unhealthy dependency. Focus on the similarities and not the differences.

These men have been a critical part of your journey back home to yourself. Without them, you wouldn't have found your way home. They were the mirrors you needed to guide you home, and your higher power was overseeing it the whole time. Should we channel Arianna again? I'm so grateful for my ex. Yes, we are grateful.

So, the first thing we do is cultivate these new habits. Daily prayer and meditation to lead us into conscious contact with our higher power. This is an essential part of Step Three, regular conscious contact with God, as we understand Him.

We change our daily habits. Exercise, eat well, and get serious about taking care of ourselves. Being emotionally and physically healthy is an enormous part of our rehabilitation. We take care of ourselves first, and then we attract someone who will follow our lead and treat us with the same care and attention. Self-love is so sexy. It's the biggest secret to getting the man of your dreams to commit to you. Go 'head, girl. You got it!

I always lost myself in my relationships and adapted to what he wanted, it's almost as if I became what he needed me to be. This is no surprise when you consider that, as a child, I had to become what my parents needed me to be to be close to them. But our higher power has given us all a uniqueness that should never be hidden. Each of us has been blessed with special and unique talents and characteristics. Going forward, we must protect and nurture them.

Your friends are one of the most valuable resources on this journey. Use them. It is essential to learn that no one person can fulfil all your needs, and that doesn't make them flawed—just human. So, you will need your friends to fill up the places he can't. Remember, friends are fantastic.

They support us, advise us, make us laugh, inspire and help nurse our wounds, but they are not your higher power; listen to them, seek advice from them, but don't take what anyone says too profoundly. Stay rooted in yourself. You don't need to spend your life explaining or trying to convince anyone of anything; it's your life. Just enjoy people and trust yourself—you and your higher power can't lose. You got this.

> "Be healthy and take care of yourself, but be happy with the beautiful things that make you you."
>
> Beyonce

In AA, they say sobriety is a daily reprieve. In other words, every day, we try to practice conscious contact with God and in so doing, we get the grace to stay transformed, but we need to put in the work. It works if you work it!

Now, please take a deep breath, channel Rihanna, and repeat after me three times:

Work, work, work, work, work, work

He said me haffi work, work, work, work, work, work

He see me do mi dirt, dirt, dirt, dirt, dirt, dirt

So, me put in work, work, work, work, work, work

See the end of the chapter for a few tips on getting started with that work, girl!

The more you practice daily habits the more you realise that you are changing at a foundational level.

Remember, it is progress, not perfection, but once I did that, I had the power for the first time to transform my life and love myself.

Today, my self-worth isn't dependent on anything outside of myself. I'm still on this journey, there is no finish line, and even though I get unsteady at times, I prioritise God, and He never fails to strengthen and stabilise me.

> "Everything depends upon our attitude towards ourselves. That which will we not affirm as true of ourselves cannot develop in our lives."
>
> Neville Goddard

Do you think it is a coincidence you have attracted this book into your life? You, young lady, are right where you are meant to be because at some point, in the quietness of your soul, you asked for more and God has provided the tools for you to get exactly that. Lasting love can be yours, and you shall get what you've always wanted. Extraordinary relationships begin with you.

Your Workbook:

Exercise 4 (Page 20)

Poetry Challenge:

Why not try to write a poem of your own? Poetry is so healing. And the constraints of the rhymes, cadences and structure bring out the best in you. Give it a go; see if you can write a few lines about *your* patterns in relationships, this could cleanse you.

Q & A

Q: How can you show up for yourself every day and create new neural pathways?

A: *Under the love and guidance of your higher power, you will create daily habits that nurture your new consciousness. These new daily habits and practices will sustain you until they become new pathways in your brain.*

Q: What can you do daily to build an infrastructure for yourself?

A: *Daily prayer and meditation. Future Self journaling. Letters to God. Daily journaling. Being still in our own presence; learning how to just be in what is; that is an embodiment practice. Learning how to be in your own presence isn't easy. We are all learning how to be in our body, learning how to change our experience of ourselves.*

Q: *What kind of affirmations can I do?*

A: *Two of my favourite embodiment affirmations are:*

I am connected to my body

I am here - Very smoky but very effective when said repeatedly

Q: How can you deepen self-compassion?

A: *Do not criticise yourself, be kind to yourself, acknowledge yourself for showing up every day.*

Q: Can you acknowledge the energy it takes to heal?

A: *Healing takes a lot of energy. The energy is starting to lay down a new network in your brain, to encourage greater plasticity. When we heal, we come face-to-face with our grief; we do a lot of different types of grieving when we heal. We grieve what never was, a need that was never met, that's grief too.*

Step 4

COURAGE

Recovering your Shadow self

Integration and self-acceptance

I'm a savage
Classy, bougie, ratchet
Sassy, moody, nasty
Acting stupid, what's happening?
What's happening?
I'm a savage, yeah
Classy, bougie, ratchet, yeah
Sassy, moody, nasty, huh
Acting stupid, what's happening?
What's happening?

– Meghan The Stallion.

Man, what a song, and what a fitting way to start the chapter. Let's use this chorus as an example of how it might look to claim and integrate your shadow self.

In this chapter, you will identify and reconnect with your shadow. In addition, this chapter aims to learn how to integrate your shadow, so you feel more whole and balanced as a person.

When we feel whole and blanked, we can allow love to enter our lives without excessive fear. This is crucial because fear leads us to sabotage our relationships and make bad choices in partners. Our psyche uses fear to protect us and keep us away from change, which is to protect us from falling truly madly deeply in love. Which is exactly what we want.

I used Meghan Thee Stallion's song Savage above, while I do not know what the writer of the song thinks about the attributes they are describing, I see it as a bold and equal claiming of the good and bad parts a person may possess.

Your shadow is a part of yourself that you'd rather not know about because it's a bit of a bitch or at least you think it is, that's why you've disowned it.

The Carl Jung talks about two types of shadows, the personal shadow, the unknown dark side of our personality and the collective shadow, which is the unknown dark side of a society.

Here, we are solely going to focus on Jung's idea of the personal shadow. Do you want to know how your personal shadow is sabotaging your relationships? Read on..

The personal shadow comprises the parts of you you hide or may not even be aware of. It is commonly referred to as your dark side; the side of your personality that contains all the parts of yourself that you don't want to admit to having.

The Shadow is a part of you, except you have decided you want nothing to do with it because you don't like it one bit. But the shadow exists and has an enormous role in sabotaging your relationships. So, read on.

I have a close friend, who was just so in love with her man it used to annoy the hell out of me. I'd be like, to myself, "why are you so dependent on him and he doesn't even treat you well, FFS, silly cow."

I felt anger towards her rising in my abdomen when she would describe his latest relationship misdemeanour, and smugly thanked my Lord I was nothing, and I mean nothing like her.

Yes, well..

Fast forward and here am I locked in a romance with a completely unavailable arsehole, and guess which girlfriend is loving me through it. Tut, tut, tut Nancy Poo.

Many moons ago, my sister once said to me, "You become what you judge, 20 years later, I get it. Perhaps we become what we judge because the only reason we judge it in the first place is that we already have it inside of us and we bloody despise it, so we push it into the shadows and forget about it. Like those flowers in the attic. Or that Parking fine that needs to be paid, you know the one you're resentful about and have been avoiding? Well, it's there needing to be paid, but you just can't face it. And so, it gets worse and worse. This is precisely how our shadow self works.

So, what would *your Meghan Thee Stallion* song be, if you were to describe yourself, warts and all? Here's mine!

I'm a savage yeh!
Sensitive, demanding, exacting
Passionate, deep & a reckless streak
Determined, lazy entitled
Ambitious, arrogant, delightful
yeh delightful! Uh!

Wow! Who knew I had it in me! I might yet have a career as a rapper... watch out Meghan Thee Stallion. Ok, perhaps not.

But you get my point, right?

Step 4 is all about doing the work, digging deep to find and reclaim those parts of you that you have disavowed because they are perceived to be not so great. The shadow contains inferiorities

But look here, anything out of balance will be functioning at a decreased capacity. Every Ying needs a Yang to be complete.

When we do not balance the light and dark within us and do so with compassion and acceptance, we are out of balance.

Ignoring the things inside of you that have been buried or pushed into the shadows will significantly limit your life and your relationships.

If an inferiority is conscious, one always has a chance to correct it.

You will never experience the power and peace that lies in fully and authentically sharing yourself with another - it's beautiful, you don't wanna miss it!

But f it is repressed and isolated from consciousness it never gets corrected and is liable to burst forth suddenly in a moment of unawareness.

That means a shrunken life and limited scope in what's available to you in love. Who wants that?!

– Carl Jung

So, go on admit it, I dare you, open yourself up to the parts of you that are truly wretched, jealous, spiteful, self-centred and self-seeking. Let's go find your shadow and see what it looks like. Don't worry, sis, it's cool. I won't judge you. We all have a shadow self. Now this is gonna be fun.

Finding or discovering your shadow isn't easy, mainly because it isn't conscious to our awareness. It is only through effort and shadow work we come to know our shadow self and discover it within us. Unlike Netflix, it is not readily accessible for viewing with a bit of self-scrolling and button pressing.

Imagine you're at a dinner party and someone asked you to describe yourself in a sentence, I'm guessing you wouldn't choose to list out all your worst traits, would you?

But you know they exist, don't you? The point is we naturally hide our negative attributes from others and even ourselves. We are conditioned to present a perfect facade to others. But facing our demons, our past hurts and buried dreams can provide a new lease of life, how?

Because bound up in our shadow selves may also be dreams and ambitions which we have buried in the burying, you get me? It's kind of like the whole baby in bathwater thing.

Now in Meghan's song above, she doesn't appear to give two hoots about being judged or perceived as good or bad.

She boldly states that one minute, she's classy, she's moody, she's nasty, and the next she's bougie. And actin' stupid, and basically what you going to about it? Nothing.

That's the point, when we claim our shadow selves, nobody cares, often we hide parts of ourselves fearing what others think - everyone is so busy getting on with their lives trying to manage their own wretched shadows they couldn't care less about yours!

Besides, you can't live your life afraid of what others think of you. I suggest you do a Meghan Thee stallion and be a savage - for me being a savage means living unapologetically do you boo!

Like us all, in her song she is describing the different aspects to her personality, some perceived good some perceived as bad.

I say perceived because depending on our family system, culture, upbringing, and many other factors, perception of good and bad traits in a person's personality can be subjective. For example, where one person sees confidence, another person sees arrogance.

Either way, in her song, we see that Meghan Thee Stallion *is* conscious of contrasting and opposite aspects within herself, and is confidently owning them, the good, the bad, the ugly. It just is what it is.

We see in this chorus an example I can work with, albeit a bit ratchet, of an integrated shadow, where good and bad can exist together in the full light of day. Where her shadow aspects are conscious, claimed and integrated.

The shadow contains inferiorities which everybody has but prefers not to know about.

The shadow is most visible when one is in the grip of anxiety or other emotions, under the influence of alcohol

One may suddenly blurt out a hostile remark during a friendly conversation

–Carl Jung

Step 4 is about 3 things:

Becoming aware of your shadow self and character flaws

Taking responsibility for them,

Accepting the parts of you, you think ain't so... how do I put this, NICE!

Step 4 challenges us to look within to discover your weaknesses and turn those into strengths.

You start the journey of self-evaluation and self-discovery so that changes can be made and mistaken beliefs can be challenged.

We may have either rejected or repressed the aspects of our personalities we do not like or that others have told us are bad. In this chapter, we get to reclaim all parts of ourselves and become whole again, as we were when we were children.

Need any more convincing? Ok, here's more reasons it is crucial to confront the shadow aspect of your personality.

It is also important to confront our shadow for health reasons; shadow aspects can assert themselves into our lives through our minds and bodies. This could give rise to mental health issues, chronic illness, anxiety, addiction, and low self-esteem.

Suppressing the shadow self can also prevent us from reaching our full potential. This is particularly true when specific character traits have been suppressed due to low self-esteem, anxiety or incorrect beliefs instilled during childhood.

Frequently, the shadow personality consists of disowned parts of your character you have deemed to be weaknesses in yourself. Your perception of what constitutes a good or bad trait will have its roots in your family of origin and their beliefs and values.

Growing up, traits such as being independent, having a sensitive nature, or not allowing yourself to show certain emotions could have been criticised or praised, depending on your family environment.

I first understood how important knowing my shadow was when I trained as a Psychodynamic Psychotherapist and encountered the work of Carl Jung, which blew my mind.

Most of us go to great lengths to protect our self-image from anything unflattering or unfamiliar. I was no different. It's done

Everybody has a shadow and unless it is embodied in the individual's conscious life, the blacker and denser it is.

—Carl Jung

much easier to observe another's shadow before acknowledging one's own shadow. I was very good at that.

During my training, seeing my own shadow helped me understand how I showed gifts in one area of life while remaining unaware of poor behaviour in others.

I was so earnest in my pursuit of love and healthy lasting relationships, but I had repressed my lack of trust, my struggle with authenticity in intimate situations, my sense of having to fight for love or my belief I do not get chosen,

Not surprisingly, I couldn't attract relationships that worked with all this buried treasure.

I didn't know how much fear I had surprised from my childhood, so I stayed stuck, never allowing love to really and enter my life.

With relationships that never took off!

Every human is susceptible to the shadow self, we all have one.

But you are reading this book to discover how to get the love you want. How to love more effectively.

Healthy relationships demand deeper self-awareness because healthy relationships demand that we stay adaptable and make necessary changes. It is not possible to make changes without self-awareness.

If we are to create health, true intimacy, excitement, space and longevity with another person, we have to face our shadow. There's no getting out of this one.

Exploring your shadow has so many benefits as I been banging on about already, but I don't want you to kiss this one!

Benefits of shadow work can lead to greater authenticity, creativity, energy, and personal awakening. There are grave consequences for our relationships if we do not address our shadow.

Most of us go into relationships ready to give our whole selves in love and have our love reciprocated. Yet when we are not in touch with our shadow, we are asleep to parts of ourselves, and we only see certain negative traits in others but rarely in ourselves.

This can give rise to a relationship dynamic of projection, on the one hand blaming the other person for things you are doing, and defensiveness on the other.

Overall, not knowing how you are driven by fear, selfishness, greed, lust, low self-worth or some other emotional or carnal drive is dangerous to any relationship - especially the one you have with yourself.

The shadow in all of us thrives on comfort zone loving, blame, victimhood, a lack of energy, joie de Vivre or creativity, codependency, avoidance, struggle to take responsibility, conflict, the list is endless, it needs these traits in you to stay it hidden from your consciousness so the shadow can gain power!

Sure, you know your bad qualities, yes, you always leave the top off the ketchup bottle, or pretend you're not home when the neighbour rings, or can be a bit bossy, but I'm not talking about the *cute* dark side.

I'm talking about the real deal devilish wretch ed, cruel and ruthless relationship sabotaging kind of dark side. The one that's so deeply rooted in you and originated in your early years. For example, a woman who chooses men who won't support her because she has such deep murderous rage and entitlement within that is unresolved. So, finding unsupportive allows her to relive her trauma because her father never gave her shit—that kind of dark side.

Knowing your dark side can help in your relationships, but avoiding it causes suffering. If we do not know the hidden parts of us, how can we understand why noise the men we do or why we are being triggered, what we desire, how to communicate our needs and wants to others effectively or even how to benefit from the energy and aliveness one gets with integrating our shadow aspects.

> *Beneath the social mask we wear every day, we have a hidden shadow side: an impulsive, wounded, sad, or isolated part that we generally try to ignore. The Shadow can be a source of emotional richness and vitality, and acknowledging it can be a pathway to healing and an authentic life.*
>
> *- C. Zweig & S. Wolf*

Ultimately, the more we suppress feelings and negative emotions into the subconscious, the greater the power they have over us. So, chop, chop, people, we got work to do.

For example, if you judge your partner for being distant, or going into his cave, it's not the distance itself hurting you. It's what you've decided his distance means about *you*. Now any healthy relationship requires that the partners have space. Can you see how this *perception* of what your partner's *behaviour means* is so destructive?

Here is my example of one of the ways my shadow showed up in my relationships.

When I noticed my partners needing a little space or distance, I panicked and thought they were cooling off me or losing interest, or that it's only a matter of time before the relationship breaks apart.

So, I would leave the relationships before they could leave me. I thought I was so strong, but I didn't have the courage to stay. To risk rejection, I was desperately afraid of love and ill-equipped to handle a serious relationship's normal ups and downs.

But for so many years, I wasn't conscious of the process happening inside me. Instead, I thought I was no-nonsense, don't tolerate any shit kind of girl. But I wasn't I was the I'm-so-afraid-you-will-hurt-me-kind-a-girl. Either way, that kind of thinking leaves a girl very lonely.

In my childhood I interpreted my father's busy-ness and infidelity as a communication that he didn't love me, I made that mean that I wasn't lovable and would not be chosen by a man unless I worked real Hard in various ways to get him and keep him.

At the deepest level, I was afraid I wouldn't be loved or I would be left. I was afraid men couldn't be trusted, so I would (unconsciously), sabotage my relationships, by leaving prematurely. I felt like the character in that Julia Roberts movie, 'The Runaway Bride.'

> How can I be substantial if I do not cast a shadow? I must have a dark side if I am to be whole.
>
> - Carl Jung

Often these deep-seated issues with self-worth are rooted in childhood and they do not belong meddling in your adult relationships. Hell, no, they don't.

They have no place sabotaging the love you have for your partner by showing up and causing disruption and bad vibes in your relationship. Dealing with your shadow self now while you are single, is the best thing you could do. You will enter your relationship armed with such deep self-awareness and you will have the tools to prevent unnecessary drama and create the most beautiful soulmate, best friend love you could only ever dream of - prior to know, that is..

Another way our shadow is destructive in our relationships is that when disengaged from our shadow, it can lead us to practice something that Jung called a' *psychological projection*'. This is when we recognise and criticise undesirable qualities in others which we hold ourselves.

When we fail to take the time to look at our own shadow, this can also lead to an obsession with the opinions of others and a lack of acceptance of our true selves.

Step 4 is all about hunting down your shadow parts and bringing its head back to the village on a stick - goodness, which was a bit strong. I guess that was my shadow speaking..

Finding ways to identify those aspects of your character which are hurting you and others is key and will allow you to have great and wonderful relationships.

What aspects of your character cause you to withdraw or walk away from love too early or too late, or to avoid love or push love away? You will find your shadow in the answer to these questions.

What causes you to stay in a relationship that is destructive and painful. Or the aspects which cause you to keep bringing the drama by apportioning blame and not taking responsibility. Aspects that keep you avoiding love, even though you want a relationship more than anything, but instead, you are living a lonely and solitary existence. The answer to these questions will help you locate your shadow.

We can learn to better understand our dark side and accept the good and bad in us. We can learn to *integrate* the divided parts of ourselves into a whole self. Ultimately this will lead us to greater peace, and wholeness and we will be more effective in our ability to give and receive love.

Step 4 suggests that we take a fearless moral look at ourselves and find all the funk beneath. Whatever works for you, but find those hidden character defects and discard them. Uncover, discover, discard.

I believe that the parts of us that are selfish, self-centred and self-seeking are such, due to legitimate fear for safety, survival and need for love rooted in our childhood. These 'unsavoury' parts of us, (and yes, you have them too), are a byproduct of certain interactions we had with people closest to us or with enormous influence or authority over us.

Where Your shadow started

Our parents, siblings, primary carers teachers or anyone in authority can make us believe that certain aspects of ourselves are good and others are not. As children, we depend on our caregivers for survival and we suppress the aspects of ourselves that are disapproved of by them while exaggerating the aspects of ourselves that our loved ones approve of

This leaves us divided, overwhelmed, inauthentic and living with an enormous hole in the soul. A hole that needs to be filled. Our shadow can only fill this hole with envy, gossip, avoidance, procrastination, project, and many other things that come from a divided and fragmented self.

In adulthood, this divided self is disconnected from our God-given compass of self-guidance, our intuition and instinct are off as we search for something outside fo ourselves to give our lives meaning. Now hands up who prepared to accept that crock of shit for a life. Hmmmm, let me have a hand count… ah, none of you. I thought not.

Remember, we are born whole and complete, but that wholeness is short-lived. The shadow is born in our childhood as a byproduct of certain interactions we had with the people closest to us.

Imagine a 5-year-old boy who knows himself and is in touch with his feelings. He is sensitive and emotional. His best friend takes his toy away and he gets mad and cries.

In response, his dad says, "Stop crying like a little girl and be a man!"

The father pushes this gentle and sensitive side of himself into the shadows and begins "acting tough." As an adult, this authentic part of him that is sensitive and emotional is deeply repressed and he has trouble feeling things, possible accessing remorse or his conscience. He will not show his emotions even when it's required. Because of that, he struggles in his relationships, never allowing himself to be seen.

Another example is a little girl angry about something and throws a tantrum. Immediately, her mom tells her to "Stop it! Stop being so bad!" Every time she gets angry, mom repeats the same thing: To stop it and be a good girl. "I must not get angry," the little girl thinks. "I have to try very hard not to get angry." With time, she dissociates from her anger — but that doesn't make it disappear.

She grows up believing she always has to "have it together." Later, she realises she has trouble at work because people push her buttons. Often, she feels like she is about to explode and doesn't know what to do. She realises her anger is there all the time, coming up in passive-aggressive ways and causing issues at work.

In diagram1 below, I have mapped out the process how our shadow self or shadow parts originate.

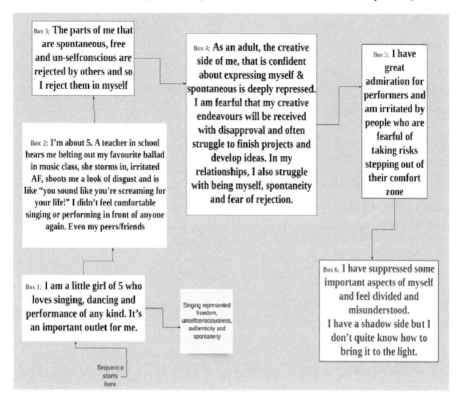

Diagram 1 shows how a teacher of mine, when I was 6 years old, had such a critical and destructive impact on me and as a result, positive aspects of myself were pushed into my unconscious and thus into my shadow.

Through shadow work in my adult life, I have been able to retrieve the traits and acknowledge how this event negatively influenced my life.

It is a huge relief to become conscious of certain fears and personality traits that hold us back and keep us hostage in our lives and discover their roots. Self-awareness is empowering and will free you up. Self-awareness will show you where change needs to be made.

What goes into our subconscious is everything we reject about ourselves — the unacceptable and unwanted bits. The minute you or someone whose love or validation you depend on says something about you is "bad," you have a reason to suppress, ignore, and deny it. Even though the shadow is unseen, it affects everything we do.

When we deny an aspect of ourselves it doesn't disappear. It just fades away from our conscious awareness. With a life of its own, the shadow can affect our actions and life experiences heavily if we don't pay attention to it.

The shadow is why we do certain things in life without understanding why we do it.

We become adults and feel we should be able to handle life better, yet we keep falling into the same unhealthy patterns. That's because the shadow operates outside of our conscious awareness, in unconscious and limiting beliefs.

The shadow contains so much potential, gifts, and talents that haven't been unearthed yet. Great things may end up in the shadow too.

Let's say that a girl is born with a strong sense of self. She knows who she is; she knows what she likes and doesn't like; she asks for what she wants and she for sure isn't afraid to speak her mind! She is a strong little girl, but she is raised in a family that constantly tells her to tone it all down because it's "too much."

The parts of her that are strong and confident are rejected, so she rejects those aspects of herself.

She grows up to be quiet, sweet, and obedient. But she doesn't understand why her life is so painful. She suppressed some important aspects of herself and therefore feels divided. She has a shadow side she doesn't quite know how to bring to the light.

That's because they have two parts of themselves operating their life and the shadow part took over when they got triggered. We often underestimate the shadow, thinking it has no power over us. But that's wrong. The shadow is very powerful!

It can turn your life upside down and destroy your most cherished relationships.

Every time you act out of your shadow, it grows bigger and bigger.

Now look at diagram 2 below and see if you can fill out the white boxes for yourself, using the yellow Post-It's to guide you. Keep referring to my example to keep you on track!

There are so many benefits of accepting your shadow self. One of the best ways to find your shadow self is to pay attention to your emotional reactions toward other people.

You might despise people who are loud, aggressive, arrogant or inconsiderate, but if you don't have those same qualities within you, you won't have a strong reaction to their behaviour

Mindfulness practice helps us recognise and accept our shadow moment by moment. Every desirable and undesirable feeling, thought, and image eventually arises in meditation, and we practice noticing and accepting them all.

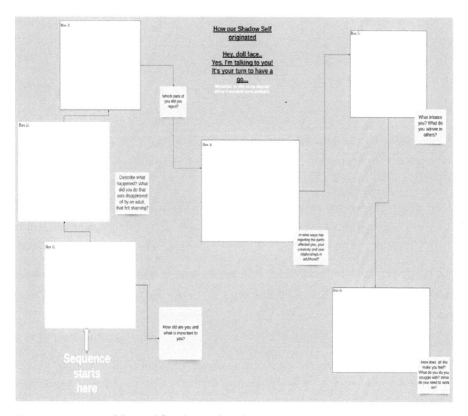

We see our anger, greed, lust, and fear along with our love, generosity, care, and courage. We gradually stop identifying with one set and rejecting the other by seeing all these contents.

We eventually see we have a great deal in common with everyone else – including those we are tempted to judge harshly. We see for ourselves why people in glass houses shouldn't throw stones."

Try to mindfully pay attention to each time someone around you does something, says something, or "is" a certain way that irritates you or upsets you.

Shadow Work

Shadow work involves getting in touch with the parts of yourself that you've repressed - or what many call your dark side. Working with a therapist with experience with this type of work is advisable, but you can try the exercises below as a gentle beginning.

There are so many benefits to shadow work. When we are not conscious of our shadow, we are dissociated, and dissociation from parts of the self creates a split. This means there is a fragmentation within you and you can experience contrasting moods and be triggered without even knowing why.

You can be like two or three people from one minute to the next, depending on whatever stimuli is in front of you triggering you. Now take a deep breath, channel Crowded house and repeat after me 3 times

Even when you're feeling warm
The temperature could drop away
Like four seasons in one day
Crowded House

This song talking about how one handles their partner's mood swings, where everything you say gets turned around, but you stick with her and stick your neck out again and get run through the mill. This is what it's like living with someone who has no idea what aspects of themselves have been pushed into the shadows from childhood. You are either extremely reactive or not reactive at all. Either way, when we are triggered, our shadow side usually comes up.

Being in a relationship with someone who is completely aware of their shadow self, is like being in a minefield, step in the wrong place. Say the wrong thing and boom. If they have repressed these aspects very deeply and have come from a family that represses their emotions as a way of being, they will be very steady, people. Not expressing their deep feelings to anyone.

Have you ever blurted out something or felt so happy one moment only to be triggered and raging in another. This is the shadow.

Or have you ever felt rage within only to be smoking and quiet, never expressing your rage? This is also the shadow.

Because your shadow is learned to suppress your authentic feelings, wishes and desires as a child. For instance, if you were scolded for having a tantrum, you may have stored that anger away and put on a more socially acceptable smiling face for the world.

By doing shadow work, you open up to the shadow you were previously resisting, you can see how your responses can often be a form of self-preservation. For instance, shutting down emotionally may have been a way for you to stay safe during childhood, though it may hinder your relationships going forward.

Doing shadow work means you get to move toward deeper integration and wholeness, which means your life is so much more peaceful and so are your relationships.

In terms of shadow work, it's also worth paying attention to what triggers you daily and why. A good place to start is paying attention to relationship dynamics, according. "Do you find yourself getting angry at certain types of conversations? Or feeling sad when seeing others succeed? These are signs of internal reactions that tell a story of your past experiences,

Shadow work will change your life. I have seen clients break patterns of self-sabotage, addiction, chronic anxiety and codependency through shadow work,"

Look at diagram 1 below and see how your shadow might be affecting your relationships.

It's important to go through the process with self-compassion, "We mustn't judge ourselves for the behaviour, but hold ourselves accountable for healing from the experience."

Diagram 1

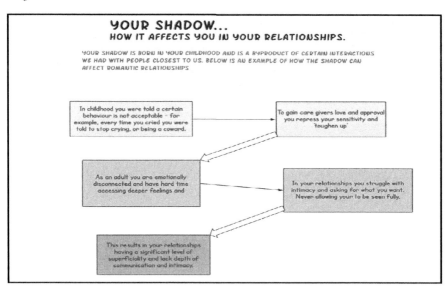

Now, have a look at diagram 2 below. I have left the boxes blank so you can have a go at doing one

for yourself. You can use these diagrams multiple times, just keep going until you feel you have seen your shadow parts more clearly. - This is an example of shadow work.

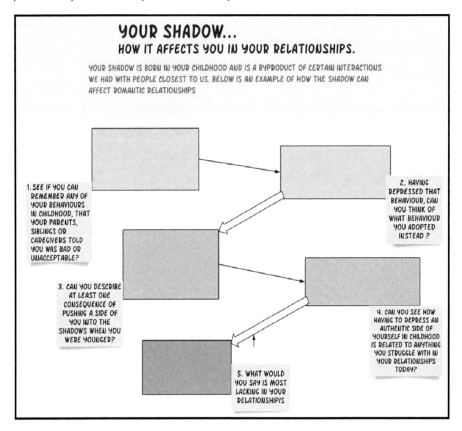

Diagram 2

The following shadow exercise is a bit lighter - You can have fun with this one. It's always surprising to see our shadow traits. Notice what bodily sensations arise out of this exercise.

Do you tense up or clench your jaw, do you find it" irritating" or enjoyable looking into yourself in this way?

If you highly value one of your positive traits, such as organised/orderly, then being around someone sloppy or disorganised can seem quite painful.

Similarly, if you highly value a trait such as modesty, it can be almost unbearable to be around a braggart. Each time you give in to these feelings of annoyance or irritation, instead ask yourself, "In what ways am I sloppy, cocky, etc.?"

Practice slowly getting in touch with those qualities you are fighting so hard to repel and push out of your experience.

We rarely enjoy surrounding ourselves with people who remind us of those qualities we claim to abhor, but there is much to be learned here.

Try looking at those experiences as opportunities for growth, self-knowledge, and self-awareness. Open yourself up to meeting your shadow self head on. It's the best investment you could make in yourself, and your relationships. Especially the hot sexy one that coming.

To attract your soulmate and find lasting love, you must first identify your shadow or know how to search for it when something is coming up for you in your relationships.

Remember, we are relational beings; we depend on others to mirror us because we cannot see ourselves or know ourselves without feedback from our environment - especially those close to us

Trying to find yourself and your shadow by reading books or doing journals is like shining a torch on your face and expecting to see it more clearly. Without a mirror, we cannot see ourselves, other people are our mirrors.

Chart 2 below is a bit of shadow work you can do by yourself. Look at my example and see if you can fill in the other. Remember to have fun and self-compassion. Self-compassion is so

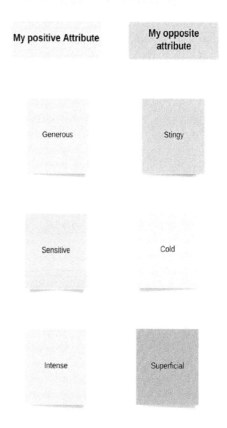

Here's Another Example of Shadow Work Something to think about..

Make a list of 5 positive qualities that you see yourself as having (e.g., compassionate, generous, witty, etc.)

Look at each positive quality that you wrote down – describe its opposite (e.g., unfeeling, stingy, dull, etc.)

Picture a person who embodies these negative qualities vividly in your mind. Roughly, this is your shadow.

My positive Attribute	My opposite attribute
Generous	Stingy
Sensitive	Cold
Intense	Superficial

important, this work is not about being critical of yourself or feeling guilt or shame. It's about deepening self-love.

Compassion is the most important thing when doing shadow work. If you become palaces with guilt, shame, regret or any other unhelpful emotion it can hinder the work one can even find oneself re-trauamtised by an even or memory when doing showed work so take it easy.

The exercises charts and diagrams are very gentle beginnings. Start with less painful memories or childhood events. If, at any time, you find this too overwhelming, get a therapist to guide you through it, someone who knows what they're doing and is accredited by a governing body.

Here is Some More Shadow work for you to try, You Sexy Thing...

Make a list of 5 positive qualities that you see yourself as having (e.g., compassionate, generous, witty, etc.)

Look at each positive quality that you wrote down – describe its opposite (e.g., unfeeling, stingy, dull, etc.)

Picture a person who embodies these negative qualities vividly in your mind. Roughly, this is your shadow.

Your positive Attribute	Your opposite attribute

Learning to Accept Your Shadow Self

Confronting your shadow self is very brave and courageous because it means looking inside ourselves at the most painful and ugly parts, which we've worked hard at hiding, even from ourselves. When we recognise and face our shadow, we can become more whole and balanced in love. All this leads to greater integration and that just means we have greater autonomy over our emotions and can therefore give and receive love more effectively.

Healing your shadow requires you love and accept all aspects of yourself, even those you judge as bad or wrong.

Unless you love yourself, you can't truly love another, and unless you accept yourself, warts and all, you will develop a dependency on the approval and validation of others.

Understanding that all aspects of ourselves — including our anger, vulnerability, conceit, and weakness — are valuable. All serve a purpose, and all aspects of us deserve our love and acceptance.

Shower your so-called dark qualities in the healing energy of love and acceptance, and they will no longer exist in the shadows. Now take a deep breath, channel Meredith Brooks and repeat after me

I'm a bitch
I'm a lover
I'm a child
I'm a mother
I'm a sinner
I'm a saint
And I do not feel ashamed
I'm your hell
I'm your dream
I'm nothing in between
You know you wouldn't want it any other way

Ahhh, so sweet is the sound of shadow integration..

It's so easy to stay unaware of our shadow self. We gravitate towards people who see us the way we want to be seen and distance ourselves from those we conflict with or clash with.

The image we have about ourselves is formed through repeated experiences with others and through self-reflection. We are inextricably linked to the world – interconnected.

People throughout our lives have given us direct and indirect information about who we are through what they see in us and how they respond to us. We then internalise these reflections from others and take what "fits" with how we would like to see ourselves and reject what "doesn't fit."

We (hopefully) form a coherent sense of identity in the world through filtering information. Even of that identity is not completely accurate and is missing vital pieces of information about who we *really* are.

There is more to the self than just what we would like to see and what we tell ourselves we are like. Carl Jung, a Swiss psychiatrist, called this the shadow. Jung wrote, "Unfortunately there can be no doubt that man is, on the whole, less good than he imagines himself or wants himself to be. Everyone carries a shadow, and the less it is embodied in the individual's conscious life, the blacker and denser it is" (Jung, 1938, p. 131).

Finding the courage to take a fearless look at yourself and become willing to clean up the mess we find. So, sister girl, Who are you? What are the messy behaviours and attitudes you are bringing with you to every relationship you get into? You don't know? Don't worry about it. We will figure it out together. The first thing you will need to do is meditate and get real still.

Once we get a clear picture of how our behaviour affected us and the men in our lives; we can get to the work of making friends with our shadow, so it has less power over us.

And so, we do the shadow work set out earlier in this chapter. This is *our version* of a fearless and moral inventory. So, we can get to know ourselves, and we can become autonomous in so doing.

Without knowledge of our character defects, we are basically fucked and so are our relationships. Without self-knowledge, there is so much blame, projection, hatred, resentment, and ill will aimed at others, including those we love. confusion about who we are, what we want and why. It is no wonder so many relationships fail and divorce rates are so high.

> "To confront a person with his shadow is to show him his own light. Once one has experienced a few times what it is like to stand judgingly between the opposites, one begins to understand what is meant by the self. Anyone who perceives his shadow and his light simultaneously sees himself from two sides and thus gets in the middle"
>
> – Carl Jung

Self-reflection and self-discovery is our most powerful tool in relationships with self and others. It is the ONE thing that will enable you to perpetually create healthy, sexy, intimate connections and bring new life to generate fresh reconciliation and intimacy regularly.

It is time you took full responsibility to change, to feel the life-affirming and transformative power that lies in self-observation and self-discovery. With renewed self-awareness, you will understand what needs to be changed.

I think, as women today, we are brave and courageous about facing our shadows and the parts of ourselves, as well as actions we take that cause us and others harm.

When I think back to my mother's generation, these women were not good at self-reflection at all. They prioritised keeping the house, cooking, and child-rearing as their main assets in relationship

I remember challenging my grandmother about her eight children with at least four fathers; she never did tell anyone the truth about how many fathers there were, but whoever, I would raise the subject, she nearly fainted right in front of me. She couldn't stand up to her own truth, to looking at herself and choices in anything less than a positive light.

Perhaps, as women, our fear of self-discovery and self-reflection, or our tendency to 'throw stones when we live in glass houses' comes from a time when women were economically and socially dependent on men. When women stayed home, bore the children and depended on her man's income, (or her man controlled her dowry), for her survival.

Perhaps our heavily prescribed and genderized existence couldn't carry the weight of too deep a scrutiny. Self-reflection would have meant becoming aware of our circumstances and would have been too painful and certainly raised up a few activists. Perhaps thesis what Jung refers to as the 'collective shadow' where the

I remember how much of of her time my mother spent complaining about my father to her mother and sister. He didn't do this, or that, or he came home so late, or he is with another woman again. I honestly don't think I ever heard her say anything much nice about the man. I specifically remember my mother complaining profusely that Dad didn't take that time to teach her how to drive properly.

> "Your task is not to seek for love, but merely to seek and find all the barriers within yourself that you have built against it."
>
> — Rumi

Our default setting is to blame men for our difficulties, limitations and painful ways our lives may have turned out. Have you ever noticed that? Think about most conversations we have as women out the men we get involved with.

Especially after a woman has had a breakup or has problems with her man?
It usually goes something like this. "He did what?"" And you mean he didn't even call you back"? "Why couldn't he tell you before?" "He's been doing this to you for years" "He's so selfish!" "Bloody men, they cannot be trusted!"

Now let us imagine each of these statements reframed and expressed from a perspective of a woman who understands that she creates her own reality and is not a victim. It would go something like this. "What do you think your reasons were for allowing him to do that? "How did you care for yourself while giving the relationship space to make some new choices?" "Could you find a way to accomplish that for yourself?," "What insights have you gained about yourself over the years with him?" "What would your life look like if you decided to no longer accept his infidelity?"

You see the difference, can you feel it? When we look at things this way, instead of blaming him, and feeling victimised, we use the experiences with him, like a 'love gym, 'to help us to get into the best emotional 'shape. 'to re orbit our thinking around ourselves and no longer around him and his actions. Whenever a conflict or problem shows up, we take full responsibility for it, what can we learn from it, we ask ourselves? What can we do to change it?

We lean in on ourselves when things go wrong in our relationships. Along with God, we become a dependable source of guidance to ourselves because we know what to do with the conflict and the pain that shows up in our relationships . We don't turn it into drama, blame, demands or criticisms, nor do we project it outwards. We alchemise it, let it bolster our self-love by turning into newer and deeper ways to express our feelings, needs and fears.

The week we can identify our shadows and flaws and become armed with the self-knowledge we need to make changes. The self-knowledge will help us discover how to give and receive love more effectively, discover the missing ingredient in some of our past relationships, and create happy, healthy, sustainable relationships going forward.

- ❖ **Project Tell the truth.** Anyone who behaves so it really annoys you, can only annoy you because you behave in that way too!

- ❖ **Treasure Hunt:** Discovering what aspects of you were unacceptable to caregivers in childhood, and therefore repressed, will lead you to buried treasure in adulthood.

- ❖ **A Melee of You-Ness:** Accepting yourself in good and in bad will lead you to deeper integration and inner peace.

- ❖ **Trigger happy:** You won't fly off the handle, withdraw, or desperately rush off to gossip about people when you discover that it isn't them, but your shadow has been triggered.

Step 5,6,7

Integrity, Acceptance, and Honesty

Recovering Integrity, Humility & Willingness

This week, we will take Steps Five and Seven together. In these chapters, you will begin the vital work of releasing yourself from your old story. Remember, 90% of transformation is letting go of our old story.

During this week, you will be focused on releasing yourself from showing up in ways that keep you in a negative relationship loop.

This means you can create new intentions, outside of your old narrative. You have the power to begin showing up differently for a future you will create —a future that is very different from anything in your past.

When our lives and relationships are under the shaping influence of old trauma/story, we are trapped in a horror story we can't escape from.

We are not free to give and receive love, nor to believe that everything always works out for our good, or to feel our worth and value. This is why these weeks ahead are a crucial component to your relationship recovery.

By recovering your integrity and a sense of belonging in chapter 5, and then embracing forgiveness of yourself and others in chapter 6, plus getting honest in chapter 7 you are releasing traumatic psychological

Week 5/6/7

In these steps we share our secrets to reclaim our integrity, and with humility and willingness, we create a new beginning in all of our relationships.

Releasing, shame, guilt and resentment is crucial if we are to uncover new, deeper ways to give and receive love just as we are.

This week, recover your integrity by sharing your secrets; you will experience a willingness to make changes and develop deeper humility.

Do not be surprised if you feel a new confidence and deeper sense of belonging.

The songs, tips and quotes are aimed at encouraging humility, self-compassion and responsibility.

Now take a deep breath, channel Jimmy Cliff and repeat after me:

I can see clearly now the rain is gone

I can see all obstacles in my way

Gone are the dark clouds that had me blind

It's gonna be a bright (bright)

Bright (bright) sunshiny day

It's gonna be a bright (bright)

Bright (bright) sunshiny day

(Which is true) I think I can make it now the pain is gone

All of the bad feelings have disappeared

Here is that rainbow I've been praying for

It's gonna be a bright (bright)

Bright (bright) sunshiny day

strongholds and reentering your relationships on completely different terms, including, and most importantly to start with, the relationship you have with yourself.

Trauma keeps us stuck in low self-worth and negative thought patterns and behaviours. It's hellish, mainly because we can't attract abundance, joy, prosperity, and lasting love if we feel like shit every day and if we don't have the belief to create our own beautiful dream life.

Our childhood trauma infects every level of our lives and thinking. Trauma is the number one reason why your relationships are not working. The number one reason why you disappear into a defensive bubble and the number one reason you cannot be present in your relationships when something that feels threatening comes up for you. Trauma is the number one reason you are defensive, reactive, needy, angry, jealous, possessive, avoidant, you name it.

Here is what Dr. Gabor Mate, one of today's renowned and leading trauma experts, has to say.

"Trauma shapes our lives. It shapes the way we live, how we live, and how we make sense of the world. It is at the root of our deepest wounds. Virtually all our afflictions, mental illnesses, physical diseases stem from trauma. Trauma distorts our view of reality and leaves us stuck in contraction, defense, and reactivity. It compromises our capacity to be in the moment, to be present to our relationships, and to fully take in the environment."

– Dr. Gabor Mate

Trauma drives us to take specific actions or accept the actions of others that we might not have if we felt safe and loved.

Sometimes we have treated ourselves or people in ways we are not proud of; we also allowed people to treat us in ways that cause the hairs on the back of our necks to stand up. Such is the power of trauma. Remember, 90% of transformation is letting go of your old story and how it limits beliefs and the possibilities you can access.

Recovering Your Integrity

(Releasing Your Demons and Reclaiming Your Angels)

These are my confessions
Man, I'm throwed and I don't know what to do
I guess I gotta give you part two of my confessions
If I'm gonna tell it, then I gotta say it all

–Usher

"Tell me, what is your deepest secret, the one you planned to take with you to your grave?" I ask provocatively.

"Pardon me?" you respond, a slight furrow in your brow now forming.

"Oh, you don't want to talk about it?"

Well, of course, you don't; nobody bloody does. Secrets carry tremendous shame, which transmutes into negative energy stored in our bodies. This causes us to feel unlovable or unworthy of good, wholesome, clean things. As if we are sullied.

This week, you will get to know the demons that have been haunting you and keeping you disconnected from your angels, yourself and others.

> "Secrets keep you sick. Keeping secrets about your shame keeps you stuck in a self-hate cycle. Everything in your spirit is screaming to express this energy, and then you consciously fight against it and push it back down. Then you feel bad about yourself for going against what your spirit wanted; more guilt, more shame, more spirit screaming to unload all that toxic energy."
>
> — Rachel D. Greenwell, How To Wear A Crown: A Practical Guide To Knowing Your Worth

In adulthood, unaddressed childhood trauma can drive your actions in negative ways and can underpin reasons you hurt others. Taking actions that have hurt others or led to other hurtful actions can lead to you living with secrets, shame and guilt.

Shame festers in the darkness of secrecy. Step Five is where we boldly face our guilt and shine a light on the darkness of secrecy.

We can only be harmed if we allow a traumatic experience or something we did to make us feel we need to hide it and keep it secret. It's a decisive move to break the silence, shatter the secrecy, and expose the truth about you and your life. We cannot let our secrets fester within us and undermine our self-esteem.

Welcome to Step Five, where we admit to God, ourselves, and another human being the truth about the secrets that have weighed us down and kept us stuck in a tremendous amount of shame. Our secrets block us from believing we deserve the good and beautiful things our hearts desire and are our birthright.

Our secrets weigh us down energetically. Ladies, come, it's time to go to confession. Here is how my confession went down when I did Step Five with my sponsor.

When I took Step Five with my sponsor, I'm not gonna lie; it was hard. It took me a while to tell all the dark secrets I had buried inside of me, to talk about all the people of different races I didn't like and the superior views I had about others, to confess my darkest secret, and I remember she sat there patiently,

> *Shame* is a powerful force. It can undermine you by making you feel unlovable. It can be exploited by others to manipulate you, bend you to their will.
>
> But shame's power is completely dependent on secrecy. As soon as the secret is let out, the boil is lanced and the burden of shame lightens.
>
> —Psychology Today Magazine

smiling gently while I twiddled my thumbs and looked around the room nervously, making polite conversation and doing occasional polite coughs. I didn't know my sponsor that well at that point, which made the whole thing harder but more relaxed at the same time.

For a while, I wondered whether I should even bother telling her the truth about me. She would never actually know, would she now?

The sobriety book *A Hunger for Healing* tells us, "The more afraid you are to tell about a certain act or thought in your Fifth Step, the more likely it is that confessing that particular thing will put a new crack in your denial and free you in a new area."

I told her I was struggling to start, and she said dismissively, in that disarming and natural English rose turned bad charm she had, "Look darlin' I've been sober for twenty-five years, but I drank a hell of a lot longer, there's nothing I ain't heard or done."

There is the time-tested saying we "are as sick as our secrets." The secrets we carry around with us weigh us down. The same secrets we promised we would take with us to our grave. Maybe we can be free, truly free from the chains of the past that haunt us.

So, I started. Talking about my prejudices, things I had done to hurt others or myself, stolen items, and people I hated, I let it all out. Step Five is about your past life. We are here moving towards a new beginning, so we must let go now. Our secrets see us sick.

As I spoke, I listened to myself in a new way. Somehow it was as if my past was becoming more real by saying it to someone else and was available for me to view it with a more discerning eye, a more forgiving heart. Because the truth is I was tired of feeling shame and guilt about what I had done.

I didn't like some of the things I was saying, but as the confessions fell from my lips, I felt so much better. My sponsor also helped me see so many ways that I was helpless or doing the best I could in those moments when I had previously judged myself as a wrong person.

I understood I was a product of a neglectful environment with parents who were so wrapped up in their pain they could not help me form a healthy and positive mindset that would lead me to make loving choices for myself and others. There is no blame here. Today, we get to clean up the mess of our past. We are not responsible for the harmful relational

> "There is no greater agony than bearing an untold story inside of you."
>
> –Maya Angelou

behaviours we inherited as children, but we are responsible for keeping them alive as adults.

I persevered with this step and told my sponsor everything; I emptied myself out. She didn't judge me, of course, she didn't, but she helped me sort through everything, what was my responsibility and what wasn't. I felt some shame when it was over, but most of all, I felt free.

Is this sounding suspiciously like a confession to you? Well, that's because it is. Confession is the practice of making oneself transparent and vulnerable. Thus, it is also the active practice of humility.

By sharing my buried secrets with another person, I released myself from the shame and guilt, which dissolved any power my secrets had over me. I realise that everyone has things they are ashamed of. I realise I am a human being. I feel such a powerful sense of belonging.

After completing Step Five with a person you trust, spend some quiet time reflecting on your experience.

Read the following promises from the Big Book of AA and consider whether they have already started to come true or are coming true for you.

Once we have taken this step, withholding nothing, we are delighted. We can look the world in the eye. We can be alone at perfect peace and ease. Our fears fall from us. We begin to feel the nearness of our Creator. We may have had certain spiritual beliefs, but now we begin to have a spiritual experience. The feeling that the [relationship] problem has disappeared will often come strongly. We feel we are on the Broad Highway, walking hand in hand with the Spirit of the Universe. (Big Book, page 75)

Choosing Someone You Can Trust to Confide In

By telling God, ourselves, and another person all the things we may have done to hurt ourselves and others, we are no longer at their mercy; we are free from the anguish that comes from living with guilt, shame, and constant self-critique. This is about humility and the individual. In sharing this, you will begin to feel accepted for who you are—a member of the human race, flawed and imperfect, just like everyone else.

You will gain a new, more profound sense of belonging to the human race and the world around you. This new connectedness will fill the unexplained emptiness you may have always felt yet not understood its root. Shame and lacking self-forgiveness keep us cut off from others, ourselves, and the more incredible world around us.

You will learn a lot about yourself in these steps, both strengths and weaknesses. The point is you will come to accept it all. For you are perfect with all your flaws and imperfections. Just the way your creator intended. So, don't sweat it. We're all in this together.

We've all heard the saying, "Our secrets keep us sick." It's the truth. But don't worry about it. It feels daunting, but remember that millions of people worldwide are getting healthy and accessible by taking this step every day, every hour, and every minute. It's not personal, it's just another growth process, and it will heal you. So, like the Nike ad says, "Just do it, girl," for we are serious about getting the love we want and that means clearing the path ahead by forgiving ourselves and others.

This may be one of the most challenging steps you will face in your Single Girls' Rehab. Still, it can be one of the most fulfilling in setting us free from the isolation we might feel before freely admitting our secrets to God, ourselves, and another human being.

But scarcely any step is more necessary to restore your sense of integration and wholeness than this one. When you experience your imperfect humanness and allow you to fully accept yourself, the good and bad, with compassion, in so doing, you allow unconditional love and acceptance to enter your life, along with peace of mind and serenity.

Because these areas are so sensitive and personal, it is essential to exercise care in choosing the person or persons we formally share our Fifth Step with. Here's what AA has to say about it:

"Such individuals should be trustworthy and somewhat detached from the situations about which we will share. For example, one would not usually call on a spouse or immediate family member to hear this confession. In fact, it is quite common to choose a therapist or pastoral counsellor for this purpose. Also, such individuals should be compassionate, not condemning."

An excerpt from Serenity, A Companion for Twelve Step Recovery, p. 45, 46

When preparing for Step Five, many people describe fear. It really can be a gut-wrenching process. Our pride wants us to feel like we're doing good and moving on from all that destructive behaviour. Step Four forces us to look back at all of that, and Step Five brings it out into the open, revealing everything.

There's also the fear that your listener will think less of you. They may have done or experienced worse things themselves, but that doesn't matter. Choose wisely and the process will go smoothly. In Step Five, the focus is you and what you've done.

> "Our secrets keep us sick is something we learn in 12 Step recovery.
>
> Finding secret keepers we can trust is the challenge."
>
> -Anon

This step is about finding someone you can trust because you will confess. There will be one person in the world who knows you, everything about you. Someone who can go back into your past with you and witness whatever you've been through back there.

Let someone of your choosing revisit the painful past with you, and as they do, they can hold you close with compassion and non-judgment. They can remind you we are not our actions or experiences. And then we let it go.

So, go ahead and find someone; it could be someone at church, a therapist, A Twelve-Step sponsor. Tell them all the things you have had in your heart, all the things you feel guilty about or ashamed of.

Leave no stone unturned. Remember, our secrets keep us sick. So, don't sweat it anymore; it's time to let them go and send them to hell.

They've had you under their shaming little grasp for long enough. Stand up and take your power back. Fuck it; whatever has happened has happened, and no one, or nothing, has the right to hold you hostage forever. Good luck.

Now, take a deep breath, channel Usher and repeat after me three times:

These are my confessions

Man, I'm thrown, and I don't know what to do

I guess I gotta give you part two of my confessions

If I'm gonna tell it, then I gotta say it all

Step Six

Recovering Your Willingness

(Willingness to Let Go of the Victim-Self)

Once we have done all this messy digging work, we are ready for Step Six. Step Six is where we are prepared to have God entirely remove our false beliefs and blind spots.

I put these three steps in one chapter because they are like one continuous step. First, we admit to our secrets, first to our personal higher power, then to ourselves and then we share with another person. Step Five is about humility and the individual, in sharing this, you will begin to feel accepted for who you are and gain a sense of belonging, filling the hole in your soul.

> *The important thing is to be able to sacrifice what we are for what we could become."*
>
> *- Charles Dubois.*

Next, after acknowledging our flaws, defects and humanness and how they have caused pain in our relationships, especially the ones we have with ourselves, we take responsibility for our part in our relationships. This is a crucial skill we must cultivate as part of our self-awareness.

Taking responsibility makes it easier to look at ourselves fearlessly. Once you understand the power of knowing all of you, good and bad, and accepting all of you with compassion and unconditional love, you are well on your way back home to yourself, on your way home to wholeness. This new, lighter, unencumbered you will notice that you are magnetising everything you want, especially the most beautiful kinds of loving relationships.

Let's look at Alanis Morrisette's classic song "You Outta Know."

And I'm here to remind you

Of the mess you left when you went away.

It's not fair to deny me

Of the cross I bear that you gave to me.

You, you, you oughta know.

If he left her in a mess, she permitted him to do so. Bottom line. Yes, of course, we want men to be kind and loving and take good care of us – and they should – but until we take good care of us first, we cannot attract anyone who will, unless he is very codependent and trying to work through his own issues by putting up with your abuse!

Bad relationships happen through us, not to us. In other words, we filter our experiences of love according to our unconscious limiting beliefs and the issues we have with self-worth. Our filter dictates our perception; we perceive ourselves as women who are not truly worthy of love for one reason or another.

If we want a different experience in love or a different type of relationship, we have to be willing to show up differently and create it. Become the change you want to see in your love life. And it's no good hating your ex; in fact, he did you a huge favour by showing the areas in you that need working on.

A recent study at UCLA demonstrated that being rejected triggers the same high alert in our brains as a primal threat—we feel like we're going to die.

Psychotherapist and author Katherine Woodward Thomas says it's because "we're flooded with these flights or fight emotions."

So, we want to kill the son of a bitch who hurt us, of course, we do, darling. But we don't because we don't want to go to jail. I mean, who will do our nails and toes?

In the Conscious Uncoupling course I took a while ago, Katherine Woodward, author and therapist, cautioned us about moving from soul mate to soul mate. We can destroy any subsequent relationships if we have not forgiven and/or released our bitterness from a previous one.

I know how easy it is to hate him after what he put you through—rejection, lies, deceit, and cruelty. But now, you have shifted from a child to an adult consciousness; you need to take full responsibility for how you showed up in your relationships.

Hands up. Who knows that you can only attract lasting love when you clean up your feelings of resentment, victimisation, and blame?

You can never take control of your life from a victimised perspective. Because a victim has no power, all her potential for healing, autonomy, and transformation lies in the perpetrator's actions. She is at his mercy. She is waiting for him to explain, hating him for leaving, mad at him for leaving her alone, expecting him to say sorry.

All this leaves you dependent on him for closure. If we are willing to begin looking at our part in our bad relationship, we are halfway to changing.

When we are willing to take responsibility for what we've experienced, and can see our part in it, we set ourselves free from the bitterness and resentment that binds us to our ex. To release these toxic emotions, we need to stop holding him responsible for the whole situation and figure out our part in the relationship's problems.

7 - Humility

Step Seven is where we change our attitude, which permits us, with humility as our guide, to move out from ourselves towards others. If we can drop our price, our need to be right, and our belief that we cannot trust in love, we can truly begin to cultivate powerful, lasting, romantic relationships. With the help of the Twelve Steps, we learn how to love ourselves and are therefore much more effective at building mutually healthy relationships.

In this book, I have utilised the main principles of the Twelve Steps to facilitate an authentic transformational recovery process from childhood abandonment wounds and relational trauma.

I have adapted the steps to heal relational wounds, rather than using the Twelve Steps for what they are conventionally known for—addiction to alcohol or drugs. Alcohol and drugs are a symptom of relational issues and disconnection from others.

Going through the steps in this book is the best decision you could make for your life. Twelve-Step programs have a worldwide membership of millions; their members experience potent breakthroughs and transformations with the Twelve-Steps.

"It works if you work it" is the Twelve-Step motto. And even though it's a spiritual programme, results, transformation, and breakthroughs happen for everyone. Those who don't believe in God simply find a God of *their* understanding, whatever that understanding is for them. I hope you can do the same.

"Humility isn't denying your strengths; it's being honest about your weaknesses."

– Rick Warren.

According to *National Geographic*, addicts in recovery experience a "psychic change" or a spiritual awakening through living the Twelve Steps.

This manifests through a behavioural transformation that makes sober living possible. In other words, the Twelve-Step program helps addicts reconnect with their spirituality and with fellow human beings.

The prayer and meditation involved in the process have been shown to connect the left and right hemispheres of the brain, realigning neurons damaged by repeated harmful behaviour. In the case of Single Girls' Rehab, which would be damaging relational behaviours such as withdrawing, lack of trust, impaired sense of self, self-abandonment, codependency, etc.

Intense emotion (such as the experience of hitting bottom or a profound realization) can create a cognitive insight phenomenon that brings the right hemisphere in harmony with the left.

Working the steps is intended to replace dependency on fear and self-centeredness with a growing moral consciousness and a willingness to submit to new higher intelligence.

The Twelve-Step program is successful precisely because it doesn't just deal with the matter at hand. When you submit to the Twelve Steps, you see that they aren't just treating your issue with men but also every problem you have with confidence, self-worth, trust, honesty, and humility. Everything.

The principles in this book recognise that a lack of self-love and self-awareness causes our problems with our relationships. By surrendering to these steps outlined here (and to a higher power), people can genuinely move on from not believing in themselves and their worth.

The problem in our relationships is one of dependency. We depend on other people to make us happy. We give our power away in our desperation to be loved. We rely on self-will to wrestle our relationships to the ground in the hope we can control them into working the way we want them to, to ease our fear and fill the hole in our soul.

So, trust this process, the prayer, the surrender to your higher power, all of it, even if you feel like this is outside of your comfort zone. I have been through it myself many times. The spiritual principles of the Twelve Steps have become a way of life for me.

Today, I am no longer a member of AA and haven't been for about 10 years, but the steps are just a way of life for me. Here's how I practice them in my life today.

- I admit when I have a problem. I am rigorously honest with myself.

- I turn it over to God. Might also seek outside help.

- I surrender. I trust God will work it out.

- I constantly look at myself unafraid, determined to see my negative flaws and dark side. I am vigilant about knowing all aspects of myself and how they might affect my relationships.

- I cultivate deep intimacy and mutual trust in my relationships, so I have a space to be authentic and confide in the people around me.

- I am completely ready to release negative traits and attributes and turn to my higher power to help me relinquish these by praying for a change in my character where necessary.

- I practice humility, getting still and spending time in silence and prayer.

- I admit when I am wrong and immediately make amends. I pick up the phone and say sorry.

- I write in a journal daily to stay humble and release difficult feelings—helps me not to blame others.

- I forgive all who've hurt me—this doesn't always happen immediately.

- I have daily conscious contact with my higher power.

- I share my experience—all that I have overcome and how the power of God has changed my life.

Twelve-Step programs and the spiritual principles contained within them offer us a powerful infrastructure. I owe it to the program. It truly changed me by teaching me how to put myself first, slow down and get reconnected to myself, educate myself about my experiences and their impact on me today, and believe that I deserve better relationships than my parents had.

> The AA motto is, "We will love you until you learn to love yourself."
>
> —AA. 12 Step Fellowship

AA's motto is "We will love you until you can love yourself."

During my 11 years of complete sobriety in AA, I learned how to have a relationship with myself. AA gave me the tools I needed to start my journey towards a healthy relationship with myself and others.

In the fellowship of AA, I learned what daily actions I needed to implement to nourish myself and deepen my connection with my higher power.

It was here that I gained a rock-solid foundation from which to begin getting to know myself and educating myself, working through my unresolved childhood issues and limiting beliefs. AA is not therapy and can only take you so far in learning about your psychology, but the fellowship and the steps provide a structural foundation upon which we build a healthy and emotional-resilient self. After these steps, you must continue to deepen your self-awareness and self-discovery. The journey towards wholeness does not end here.

It was in AA that, for the first time ever, I understood that I had emotional issues lying beneath the problems I was experiencing in my relationships.

After AA, I went to therapy for eight years in one stint. Then, of course, I trained to be a therapist. Today, I will always check in on a therapist or coach wherever issues pop up that I might be struggling to work through.

I don't agree with everything in the program, but, as they say, look for the similarities and not the differences. When it was time for me to leave, I did so, but I will always respect the program's core principles. They work. They free you from the shackles of codependency, low self-worth and self-abandonment. You will be free to start your journey towards healthy, loving, communicative and reciprocal relationships.

Now take a deep breath, channel Mary Mary and repeat after me:

Take the shackles off my feet so I can dance

I just want to praise you

I just want to praise you

You broke the chains now I can lift my hands

And I'm gonna praise you

I'm gonna praise you

The Big Takeaways

- **Who Is Underneath There:** Trauma shapes the way we live, how we live and our view of the world.

- **Secrets Keep You Sick:** Find someone you can trust to tell your deepest darkest secret/s to.

- **Poor Me, Pour Me, Pour Me a Drink:** You are not a victim. Take responsibility for your part in every painful relationship you ever had.

Step 8,9

RESPONSIBILITY & LOVE

Recovering Love

(Scared People Hurt People)

I often say to my daughter, as my mother used to say to me, "Stop saying you're sorry, just don't keep doing it!"

The best apology is changed behaviour. But you know that already, right?

This week, we are looking at past behaviours and how they damaged our relationships with other people.

When we go through making amends to those we have hurt, we clean our energetic field of toxic feelings like guilt, shame, self-blame and victimisation. Without these energetic barriers holding us back from love, we set ourselves free to connect more deeply with others.

By recognising our part in the conflicts and struggles we have experienced in our relationships where possible, we get to let go of being a victim and instead take responsibility.

We may not have handled past grievances or conflicts in our relationships in the best way.

Mostly, we did not have the tools to deal with difficult relationships.

Stuck in low self-worth, victimhood, blame or self-centredness, we may have hurt people close to us without meaning to do so.

Here, in Step Eight, we look at past behaviours and how they have damaged relationships with other people.

We prepare to make amends where necessary and

Week 8/9

This week, we recover the courage to love again. Self-love takes courage, be courageous.

So many of your experiences have made you afraid to boldly claim the love you deserve and falsely led you to believe that you are unworthy of love.

Taking responsibility for our past actions by making amends to those we have hurt, including ourselves, is the best thing we can do for ourselves.

The songs, quotes and tips aim at you becoming aware that you may carry feelings of guilt, shame and resentment, which have frightened you into playing small.

Now take a deep breath, channel Kelly Clarkson and repeat after me three times:

Because of you I never stray too far from the sidewalk

Because of you

I learned to play on the safe side so I don't get hurt

Because of you

I find it hard to trust not only me, but everyone around me

Because of you

I am afraid

I am afraid

begin to make positive changes in dysfunctional relationships by discovering what part we have played in them. We will make amends to those we have hurt, including ourselves, and move on with our lives.

We no longer sit in self-blame, shame or fear about hurt we have unwittingly caused to others. We've done that for way too long. We are over it. If we hurt another, we are truly sorry; if they hurt us, we fully forgive; if they're still mad, that's their issue. We are moving on. Time to let that shit go.

Step Eight asks us to make a list of all the people we may have harmed along the way, and then be prepared to make amends to those people.

We can do this face-to-face, by writing a letter or even making a living amends, which means we change our behaviour.

Looking at past behaviours and how they damaged relationships with other people and preparing to make amends wherever possible and necessary is a very powerful and hopeful way to begin working on the relationships you value or perhaps revisiting a relationship you have written off.

You can begin to make real positive changes in dysfunctional relationships by discovering what part you have played and being willing to take action towards healing the relationships with the others involved or just within yourself.

Becoming willing to make amends to those harmed is not always easy or possible, but it can be a very humbling and powerful growing experience to admit wrong-doing, especially to the person harmed. It brings much relief where possible and can help those trying to recover from so much guilt!

> "The thing about a hero is, even when it doesn't look like there's a light at the end of the tunnel, he's going to keep digging, he's going to keep trying to do right and make up for what's gone before, just because that's who he is."
>
> — Joss Whedon

Step Eight leads you to the knowledge that some things you can change and some things you can't change. No matter how humble or willing we may be, we cannot control other people; we can only do our best to make amends where possible.

By identifying who you've harmed and how you've harmed them and then making a list, you begin to radically shift your energetic and relational fields. Even if you never get to make amends in person, that you are writing this down is shifting so much for you already.

Now is the time to be open and honest. Think about any instances of selfishness, greed, dishonesty, negligence and so on, regardless of whether you intended to cause harm at the time.

Step Eight is a wonderful step for beginning to rebuild some bridges that were burned in your past relationships.

When my childhood trauma had its grip on me, some of my relationships with loved ones became strained, and I hurt some of those closest to me.

I was afraid, mistrustful, impatient, demanding and selfish. Such was my emptiness and need for love and safety, I really didn't think so much about others. I didn't have the capacity.

This step gave me the chance to reflect on my past and take full responsibility for my part in the burned bridges.

Thankfully, all the previous steps brought me to a place where I could honestly sit down and create a list of the people I'd harmed and become willing to make amends.

Step Eight is based upon the principle of authentic love.

Steps One through Seven were more personal steps as their focus was more on my past thoughts and actions that caused me to make some internal changes.

Step Eight asked me to continue making changes by revisiting my past and making a list of those I'd wronged somehow. In addition, I was preparing my heart to become willing to make amends to such people in Step Nine. Yes, girl, if you can, make amends to all those people you have hurt.

I recall one night calling up four of my exes and just apologising for the way I had behaved. Cutting one off. Changing my number on another who did something I didn't like. Saying some hurtful things to another ex, who wouldn't yield to my demands for deeper commitment.

> "The thing about a hero, is even when it doesn't look like there's a light at the end of the tunnel, he's going to keep digging, he's going to keep trying to do right and make up for what's gone before, just because that's who he is."
>
> — Joss Whedon

I listened to these men as they told me how they perceived our relationships and how they felt. For the first time without my "fear muffs" on, I really listened to the other side of the story. I braced myself and just listened; I was curious to hear how things were for them and learn about me. Boy, did I learn a lot about me.

I had to become willing to offer my apologies to those I'd hurt and extend a good dose of authentic love. This required humility and trust that such actions would help me in my future to make love and not fear a priority in my relationships. But I could not prioritise love without a higher power to give me the strength to trust that I had everything I needed within me, that I always had myself and my higher power to fill me with love, peace and a sense of safety.

Now, this step wasn't easy. Owning my selfishness and taking responsibility for hurting others was painful. It's easier to point fingers at others or just look the other way.

It's easier to let the past be the past. But when I really humbled myself and honestly went inside on this matter, I realised I was carrying around guilt and shame. The people I'd hurt did not deserve it, and I knew if I wanted to continue to grow personally and spiritually, I had to be willing to make amends and do the right thing.

Seeing this list helps you understand the impact you have on the world around you and your responsibility, and it will hold you accountable for dealing with it. And that willingness to make amends will do your heart the world of good.

We must get help to confront false beliefs about ourselves and others as these beliefs will destroy our relationships. Here are two examples of false beliefs I held for so long.

Releasing False Beliefs, Forgiving and Opening Up to New Love Again

My Dad Didn't Love Me

When we show up negatively in our relationships, there is always a painful belief about ourselves at the root. I thought I would share how I held on to a false belief about my father and how this belief showed up in my relationships, causing blocks and ultimately blocking me from any love. This belief prevented me from having full and loving relationships for most of my life.

I had a session with a powerful coach once. I told him I was struggling with the coaching program I had enrolled onto, that I wasn't getting the clients and found myself not keeping up with the work. As much as I wanted success, I couldn't seem to perform and show up for myself.

You are about to witness the power of coaching, why I became one and why I highly recommend you work with one too.

I told this coach that I felt I wasn't getting the promised results.

He said to me, "Have you done the modules we set out?"

I said, "Well, I've done some of them, not all."

He responded, "Well, on a scale of one to ten, how far would you say you are in terms of the work we set and the work you've done?"

I said, "Err, about fifty per cent," but in truth, it was a four.

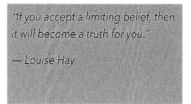

"If you accept a limiting belief, then it will become a truth for you."

— Louise Hay

He said, "So, why do you think you've only done about fifty per cent of the work we set out for you to do, knowing that if you follow our guidance, you will be thriving on this course and getting the results you say you really want?"

I thought about it for a minute; I hadn't asked myself why I wasn't doing the work set out by him, especially as I had paid him to do this course. I said, "Well, I've done the modules I think I need most to get the results I want and I've kinda skipped the others. I'm cherry-picking the models I believe will be most helpful to me."

Amused, he peered at me and said, "Okay, so what's the issue with trust? Who is it in your life that you couldn't trust?"

The question took me somewhat aback as I hadn't overtly mentioned anything about trust.

But then again, I had.

His question touched something within, and I felt my eyes welling up before I had even connected to any specific memory. I thought about it for a while, then responded.

"It was my dad," I said.

Coach nodded. "And what is it you couldn't trust about him? What did you feel about him?"

The tears were now kind of streaming. "I felt like he didn't love me," I said.

"And what's the memory that makes you think that?" Coach asked.

I immediately knew. I vividly remember an incident with my father, even though it was at least 40 years ago. I described the event to my coach.

"Once, my mother brought him this massive plate of dinner she had meticulously prepared and laid out for him. Dad was a very particular ex-army type and incredibly precious about his dinner.

"Life has no limitations, except the ones you make."

— Les Brown

"I begged her to let me take it into him, in his office, and so she carried it to his office door and gave it to me to take into him."

"How old were you?" Coach asked.

"About six, I replied."

Ryan nodded again. "Okay, so what happened?"

"Just before I proudly strolled into his office, I took a bite out of his potato. I wasn't hungry at all; I just wanted to feel I could cross a line with him that no one else would dare to. When I handed him his plate, he roared at me so loudly and angrily as if I had committed the worst crime. As if I had infected his food with my bite. I felt very small. I felt ashamed and worthless. I was devastated."

"And what decision did you make there and then? What meaning did you give that?"

I thought about it for a minute, then responded. "I felt my dad didn't love me." More tears.

"And what did you decide to do about it?"

"I decided I was going to make him love me!"

"And how were you going to do that?" he asked.

"I was going to be the smartest, cleverest, most attractive and funny woman possible and then I would get his attention. Then I could make him love me."

"And that's what you're doing right now on this call; remember you said at the beginning of the request that you needed some attention?"

"Gosh, yes," I said.

"So, you see, it's just a belief, and that belief has been disempowering you for so many years, making you not trust and try so hard to get attention and still, in the end, it's impossible to believe that you are loved. But it's not true; your dad did love you. You just made it up that he didn't. He did love you."

This information blew my mind. I started to tell him all the loving things my dad used to do and how in his death, he left me his most prized possessions. I was the only person he showed love to with such a huge gesture. I believe I was the only person he trusted.

> "There are so many things we've been brought up to believe that it takes you an awfully long time to realize that they aren't you."
>
> — Edward Gorey

He said, "You see, it's just a belief, a false belief." That conversation changed so much for me.

When I looked back at my relationships for the first time, I could see how that six-year-old girl had never grown past that moment when she decided she wasn't loved and had to 'make' people like/love/notice her.

I reflected on my past relationships, and the truth began to dawn on me what my story was: I'd only ever met untrustworthy men who were unavailable to love me, and that's why I didn't succeed in my relationships.

I had met so many men who wanted to be available to love and take care of me and who could see me for all I was, but because of my debilitating six-year-old-girl belief, I was living in a loop where I was unloved and needed to work hard to be loved because that was my comfort zone in relationships. Choosing men incapable of loving me meant I would never be loved the way I wanted anyway.

I would try way too hard to be loved or be super demanding for their attention and their love. I believed love should be expressed and demonstrated to make ME feel good without considering what they needed. My favourite phrase for most of my life was, "If that were me, I would never do that to you! Why can't you just say, 'I'm sorry,' or explain how you feel?"

I was always so desperate to have effective, meaningful communication (but meaningful and effective according to who?). I forgot that everyone is different and has his own way of expressing himself. I forgot that what seems like negligible effort from my lover in my mind might be considered an enormous effort in *his* heart and mind.

It took me a long time to figure out that people were not going to love me in the way I expected them to, but if I could drop my fear and lack of trust for a minute, I could see the many concrete ways they were demonstrating their love and commitment.

My dad had passed away many years before this interaction. So, my coach told me to write a letter to my dad, telling him all the good things I remembered about our relationship and how special he was to me.

I took my time and wrote the letter. Afterward, I wrote down all the false beliefs I was beginning to see in myself with the help of my higher power and the support of my coach.

Step Four is about courage, the courage to look at ourselves and the limiting beliefs that are blocking love from our lives; to take action to change them by getting help from someone who can help us shed these damaging, limiting beliefs.

I Wasn't as Strong, Talented or as Beautiful as My Sisters

Another limiting belief from childhood that caused damage in my adult relationships is to do with my siblings. As the youngest, I found it hard to forge my identity and voice compared to my sisters. They were strong characters. I bestowed these superpowers onto them, assuming they were stronger, prettier, smarter—we all have our own unique strength, beauty, and talent. I know that now.

Still, it was a long time before I could crawl out from beneath their shadow and realise that I had so many gifts of my own.

As I grew up, the way I related to my peers and romantic relationships was impacted by my relationship with them.

I seemed to constellate the same old dynamic whenever I came across people with strong characters or who I thought were smarter or prettier or anything-er, I'd just shrink.

> "When you feel like you are less than others, then you are right."
>
> Anon

I would automatically become the 'little sister' again who didn't think she was enough.

Nothing is more painful than being estranged from your flesh and blood,

especially in a world where good friends are hard to come by.

Much like our relationships with parents, our relationships with siblings are as damaging and impactful in shaping the unhealthy ideas we hold about ourselves.

Freud believed that sibling relationships are based upon "primal hatred" and "unfathomably deep hostility."

Is it time to release yourself from the person you were with your sibling and be free to love as your highest self.

Our false beliefs can also be created through our relationships with our siblings, it's not always parents as some might imagine.

The thoughts we have towards our siblings play an essential role in our emotional life and can influence the development of negative feelings of low self-worth and self-esteem if we do not have a positive relationship.

I always felt locked out of my relationship with my siblings. I felt bullied and alone.

Another example of a deeply entrenched false belief I had about myself was to do with my siblings. My father bought me a large three-bedroom apartment in an affluent part of central London when I started university.

He didn't buy my siblings anything, and they were deeply distressed about it. They blamed me, and I took the blame. Why? I guess it was already a family pattern. I had indeed seen it in my mother and her relationship with Dad.

I struggled, with guilt, with low self-worth, to reconcile my living in such luxury while my father told me that "they were on their own now."

I lived in such misery and was only truly happy when I didn't interact with them. If I had to buy something for me, I had to get it for them too, otherwise, I felt guilty. I'd even lend my sister money and then borrow from my friend. I was asset rich and cash poor, relying wholly on my dad's inconsistent and conditional allowance.

Nevertheless, I lived in my beautiful apartment and did my best to feel okay with it, and eventually, I made peace. I couldn't live with the guilt forever. If my sisters or brother wanted something, it was their responsibility to approach our father. Not my problem. They should contact Dad and sort it out with him, not blame me. I put the matter to bed. Or at least I thought.

> When you believe what you have and how you were raised keeps you from having everything you ever dreamed of, you are right.
>
> – Anon

I lived in that flat for 15 years and finally sold it. I was very resistant to letting it go; I only agreed to sell it because the service charges were so high and it was becoming way too expensive for me now that I had started my training as a therapist.

One sunny afternoon in Belsize Park, my silver-haired art-collecting analyst pointed out how interesting it was that after 15 years in that three-bedroom apartment, I always had two female flatmates occupying the rooms even though I could afford to live alone. Somehow I had unconsciously mismanaged my money to the degree I had to rely on lodgers to sustain me.

We explored it further and realised that these two lodgers represented my sisters, all the while I thought I had resolved the issue in my heart and mind and let them go.

I was still living with my sisters somehow and hadn't resolved anything. I was still trying to compensate for something that was never my problem initially and depriving myself of my lovely home and my right to enjoy it.

The truth is that these female lodgers helped me unconsciously alleviate the guilt and self-loathing of having something they didn't. I couldn't claim my power and declare my right to what I had been given.

Due to the influence of my sibling relationships, I spent 20 years trying to make up for their pain.

This is codependent and disempowered behaviour, and I can assure you if I was showing up in my home this way, I was showing up disempowered in all areas of my life. If the root is infected, so are the fruits that emanate from it.

Feeling responsible for others, taking on other people's problems, neglecting my right to be happy; all this behaviour kept me stuck in not enoughness.

"We are all lies waiting for the day when we will break free from our cocoon and become the beautiful truth we waited for."

— Shannon L. Alder

I was addicted to not being enough. I judged myself as being constantly wrong, selfish, greedy, weak, etc. These were the labels I put on myself.

And it was showing up in my life. I could never quite measure up; always creating conditions in my life that meant I fell short of getting what I wanted. Like doing my dissertation the night before it was due or getting lots of parking tickets so I wouldn't have the cash to buy what I wanted. More drama meant I had to live with the consequences of never measuring up—and therefore never being enough.

These are two compelling examples of what can lie beneath our issues in relationships. They have their roots in our family of origin and if we don't stand up for ourselves and take responsibility for our right to happiness and truth we will remain at the mercy of the residue these experiences leave on our lives and influence who we show up as in our relationships.

When we are not free to be the highest versions of ourselves, everything will suffer without past traumas meddling with our ability to give and receive love.

The minute we practise looking within, listening to the feedback from people we trust and having the courage to release the lies we believed about ourselves that we were not loved, or strong, or worthy, in that moment that we release these lies, we can claim our happiness and our right to be loved.

This is the moment when you realise that everything you have in your life, and everything you lack in your life, is all created by your beliefs—nothing more, nothing less. So, girl, it's time. Time to get what you want. Are you ready to *go create it?*

Haven't had a dream in a long time

See, the life I've had

Can make a good man bad

So, for once in my life

Let me get what I want

Lord knows, it would be the first time

Lord knows, it would be the first time

Step 9

DISCIPLINE

The Promises Go 'Head, Girl, You've Earned It

And so, we make direct amends to such people we have hurt wherever possible, except when to do so would cause them injury or harm. We repair any damage caused where possible and we are prepared to forgive those who have hurt us.

Equally important, and perhaps the most important of all, we must be prepared to make amends to ourselves and forgive ourselves for any harm we have caused to ourselves and our relationships.

> "There is no shortcut for hard work that leads to effectiveness. You must stay disciplined because most of the work is behind the scenes."
>
> — Germany Kent

Your amends can come in different forms; you decide how you want to do this. Below is a rough guide, but you choose what works for you in the end. Even if you only ever say a prayer for the person you feel you have harmed and ask for forgiveness plus forgive yourself, it is amends.

Tip:

After making a thorough list, many people find breaking it up into four categories. Be creative and do it your way. Ask our higher power for guidance.

Amends to be made now to the person directly or by letter.

Partial amends (to avoid harm or injury to others).

Amends to make later, whenever it feels appropriate.

Amends that may never be made in person—a letter will suffice, perhaps a prayer with a letter that is never sent.

You can also tell another your story about how you feel you hurt someone; this is also a type of amends.

The important thing is not to get bogged down by this; do your best and move on.

For some, this can take a very long time, months or even a year, but you shouldn't rush it. Other people who have completed this task might tell you how freeing it is, and while that may be true, trying to take a shortcut is only limiting the power that this step will bring to your recovery.

So, we have reached the end of Steps Eight and Nine and are approaching our final chapter. You have done wonderfully to get this far. You are changing, no doubt. Now, take a deep breath, channel Jennifer Hudson and repeat after me three times:

Look at me
Look at me
I am changing
Trying every way I can
I am changing
I'll be better than I am.
I'm trying
To find a way
To understand.
But I need
I need a hand

The Rewards of Releasing the Past

Ladies, we are releasing the past. Below is one of the readings from the Big Book of Alcoholics Anonymous that I love the most.

If we are painstaking about this phase of our development, we will be amazed before we are half way through.

We are going to know a new freedom and a new happiness.

We will not regret the past nor wish to shut the door on it.

We will comprehend the word serenity and we will know peace.

No matter how far down the scale we have gone, we will see how our experience can benefit others.

That feeling of uselessness and self-pity will disappear.

We will lose interest in selfish things and gain interest in our fellows.

Self-seeking will slip away.

Our whole attitude and outlook upon life will change.

Fear of people and of economic insecurity will leave us.

We will intuitively know how to handle situations which used to baffle us.

We will suddenly realize that God is doing for us what we could not do for ourselves.

Are these extravagant promises? We think not. They are being fulfilled among us—sometimes quickly, sometimes slowly. They will always materialize if we work for them.

3rd ed. Big Book pg. 83 & 84

Step nine is another one of the twelve steps that initially appears most difficult, but the rewards of putting this principle into practice can be immense. The spiritual principle involved is that of forgiveness, not only of others but forgiveness of self, which can bring healing to both parties.

> "Everyone thinks of changing the world, but no one thinks of changing himself."
>
> Leo Tolstoy

We are now able to benefit from the promises that our commitment to these steps has yielded. After working through the 12 Steps, I met the man I wanted to spend the rest of my life with, got engaged and had a baby. I completed a masters in Feature Film screenwriting, wrote a movie and become a licensed psychotherapist. I bought a wonderful home. Although I am no longer a member of and 23 step program I owe a lot to them. I got the tools to begin my self-love journey along with so many blessings. These are the promises.

Today, I am not with my ex-fiancé anymore. But we have the most incredible, beautiful and vibrant little girl called Camilla, she is my spirited and unique soul mate. Her father and I co-parent in a way that most people cannot believe. We are fully committed to her happiness and healthy emotional development. I have two stepchildren, Camilla's older sister and brother, whom I will always love, no matter what has passed and what the future may bring.

The steps changed my life forever. They were my first look into self-discovery and self-love. I continue to possess and deepen the tools to build safe, authentic, sexy and happy relationships and to always take responsibility and apologise swiftly when I am wrong if the situation permits.

I have never been happier and have never had a closer relationship with God. I am blessed beyond words and grateful beyond expression. Today, I live a life of authenticity, faith fearlessness and integrity. My relationships are beautiful. Honest, open, committed, full of acceptance and a source of strength and a place from which I can flourish. Now, can I get an amen from the people at the back?

Now take a deep breath, channel Yolanda Adams and repeat after me:

I say a prayer every night
Whatever I do, I'll get it right
With no regret, no guilt or shame this time (no not this time)
Once I surrender, I won't dare look back
'Cause if I do, I'll get off track
Move ahead in faith
And patiently await your answer
What will it be?
Sight beyond what I see
You know what's best for me
Prepare my mind, prepare my heart
For whatever comes, I'm gone be ready
Strength to pass any test
I feel like I'm so blessed
With you in control, I can't go wrong
'Cause I always know
I'm gonna be ready

The Big Takeaways

- **Sorry the Hardest Word?** Making amends is a powerful way to release yourself from guilt, shame and resentment.

- **What a Wonderful World.** We are promised a wonderful world if we commit to a process of self-reflection, self-development and self-discovery.

- **Enough Is Enough.** Somewhere along the line, you made a decision that you were not enough, then set up your life so you would never measure up.

Step 10,11,12

DISCIPLINE, GROWTH AND SERVICE

Recovering Freedom through Discipline

In this final week, we acknowledge the call. The far-off call that says it is time to experience emotional fulfilment by recovering freedom through discipline.

We address the fact that self-love requires action be taken on a daily basis. We surrender to living a spiritual life, softening away from fear and moving towards deeper self-awareness and education.

Continuing to do anything in our daily lives usually means that we get better at it and so it goes with Step Ten. As you may have discovered whilst doing your shadow exercises, we don't enjoy admitting to being wrong, it's much easier to blame others.

Capacities we have developed through reading and doing the work in this book.

The quotes, music and tips are aimed at encouraging greater self-discipline, to implement daily spiritual practices in our life.

Resistance is understandable; we are not used to trusting God so deeply. We are not accustomed to believing that God's will for us and our inner desire for lasting love and a soul mate could coincide. It is the inner commitment to follow our dreams that triggers the support of the universe.

Now take a deep breath, Channel DMX and repeat after me,

We're just children that act grown

There is so much we're entitled to

Yet, we receive so little

Admitting when we are wrong and promptly being accountable for our side of the street is necessary to maintain healthy relationships. Pride and stubbornness in relationships do not allow us to deepen intimacy.

Because this time in our spiritual warfare

We are comfortable in the middle (alright, yea)

So I pray that you open our eyes (yes)

Give us the anointin' to recognize the devil and his lies

If we keeps our actions wise, our prayers sincere

Our heads to the sky, you will diminish our fears

In Jesus' mighty name, we are brave, amen

The best part about practicing the Tenth Step in your daily life is that the more you are exercising self-discovery, honesty, humility and reflection, the fewer apologies and amends you have to make! Not to mention the greater degree of inner peace you feel.

I used to despise the word discipline. For me, it felt like someone was trying to put a straitjacket on me. It was counterintuitive. I came from a family that lacked emotional literacy, but I had everything I wanted financially.

For some people, and I was one of them, not having to work for stuff or pay bills means never exercising their discipline and follow-through muscles. If we wish to grow, we must accept that growth and evolving beyond old patterns requires discipline to help us implement new habits and practices in our lives. Discipline is a must if we are to succeed here.

When I look back at my younger years, I realise how idle I was. On my summer breaks from university, I'd sit back and smoke weed with my feet up in our lush summer house in America.

Mostly I did little else, just contemplated what colour Victoria's Secret underwear I would buy at the mall the following day. I mean, Ricky was over most days. I had to make sure I was prepared!

Now, take a deep breath, channel Bruno Mars and repeat after me three times.

Today I don't feel like doing anything
I just wanna lay in my bed
Don't feel like picking up my phone, so leave a message at
the tone
'Cause today I swear I'm not doing anything
Nothing at all
Woo, ooh, woo, ooh, ooh
Nothing at all
Woo, ooh, woo, ooh, ooh

> "For a scientist, this is a good way to live and die, maybe the ideal way for any of us - excitedly finding we were wrong and excitedly waiting for tomorrow to come so we can start over."
>
> — Norman Maclean

It's true that growing up with money and lush houses and holidays was excellent.

But I had also just lost my mum to cancer, and no amount of money can ease the pain of a teenage girl losing her mother. I was also paralysed by fear and the limiting belief I wasn't enough.

Sure, I went to university and got my degree, I managed to do quite a bit despite the fear and low self-worth that stemmed from my childhood. But I didn't have ME, I was estranged from myself. I wasn't cultivating a kind, loving relationship with myself. I just didn't know how to until I entered AA where my journey began. Through AA, I got closer to my higher power and practices like self-reflection, discipline, responsibility, and prayer.

So, many of us believe that money, or finding our soul mate, or having children will fix us; in my 10 years as a clinician, a mother, a sister and a partner, I've learned that the only thing that can heal your life (you don't need fixing, you're not broken) is embarking upon a journey of self-discovery and spirituality. This will help you to soften away from depending on outcomes in love and having so many expectations.

Walking the spiritual path reminds you that you already have everything you need inside of you. People, places and things require discipline.

Having self-discipline and perseverance is almost counterintuitive for some of us. The self-discipline required to walk a spiritual path calls on us to do certain things regardless of how we feel.

We need to make sure we are spending time in prayer and meditation, or just sitting in stillness and doing breathwork, or journalling, even if we're tired, busy at work or play, or even when filled with despair.

We practise spiritual principles because we understand that those things are the actions that will help ensure our continued self-development.

Spiritual principles, such as prayer, inventory, amends, and forgiveness, will lead us closer to knowing ourselves and having peace, giving us the ability to love more deeply and have healthier relationships.

Many of us could not have any long-term relationship, or if we did, it was not any kind in which we resolved our conflicts in a healthy and mutually respectful way.

Whether it was raging fights with people who never spoke of the underlying problem that caused the fights or not standing up for ourselves and being conflict avoidant because it seemed easier to burn a bridge rather than work through a problem and build a stronger relationship, these are all parts of continuing to take our personal inventory to reveal our greatest liabilities and assets. But it's not always easy to know when we're wrong, especially if we are relatively new to this work.

> *Pride is pride not because it hates being wrong but because it loves being wrong: To hate being wrong is to change your opinion when you are proven wrong; whereas pride, even when proven wrong, decides to go on being wrong."*
>
> *— Criss Jami, Healology*

We become more proficient at figuring out when we're wrong with the consistent practice of taking a personal inventory. We use Step Ten to maintain a continuous awareness of what we're feeling, thinking, and, even more importantly, what we're doing.

Taking a personal "inventory" in Step Ten means taking stock of your emotional disturbances.

Knowing yourself is an important step to achieving happiness and peace. To learn your true self, identify the qualities that make you unique. Daily reflection and meditation can help you cultivate a deeper understanding of your identity; taking personal inventory is a form of daily reflection and meditation.

As time goes on, you can build on these discoveries to create a deep and meaningful relationship with yourself.

QUESTIONS FOR PERSONAL INVENTORY

These questions can address the general areas we want to look at in a personal inventory:

Learn to be honest with yourself. Knowing yourself means recognising different parts of your identity, personality, and being. The goal is not to criticise yourself but to acknowledge all sides of your personality. Open to the possibility of learning new things about yourself.

When you evaluate yourself, pay attention to what makes you feel uncomfortable. These emotional signals can tell you if you are trying to avoid a subject.

Are you insecure about that characteristic? If so, what can you do to overcome it?

For example, if you don't like to look in the mirror, ask yourself why. Are you insecure about your looks? Are you worried about your age? Then, you might consider whether this is a fear that you can conquer.

Ask yourself thoughtful questions. This knowledge can help you realise what makes you happy or stressed. You can use this information to help you spend more time on activities and goals productive for you. Some questions you can ask include:

- What do you love doing?
- What are your dreams in life?
- What do you want your legacy to be?
- What is your biggest criticism of yourself?
- What are some mistakes you've made?
- How do others perceive you? How would you like them to perceive you?
- Who is your role model?

Step 11

SELF-AWARENESS LEADS TO GROWTH

Self-Awareness Leads to Growth

Step Eleven tells us to seek daily conscious contact with God through prayer and meditation. We do this because we are seeking a journey beyond us. We understand that embarking on an inner journey will lead us to growth and happier, more effective ways to love. The goal is to love unconditionally and not be attached to outcomes in love. We already have everything we need within ourselves.

> "Until you make the unconscious conscious, it will direct your life and you will call it fate."
>
> — C.G. Jung

Well-being and feeling fulfilled must be cultivated through daily practices. Prayer is my go-to every time! Prayer may elicit a relaxation response, along with feelings of hope, gratitude, and compassion—all of which have a positive effect on overall well-being.

All prayers are rooted in the belief there is a higher power that has influence over your life.

This belief can provide a sense of comfort and support in difficult times—a recent study found that clinically depressed adults who believed their prayers were heard by a concerned presence responded much better to treatment than those who did not believe.

The more we pray, the more we experience God's presence on the inside of us; this means we have peace and feel a sense of awe each day as we watch miracles unfolding in our lives.

In the final steps, we understand that discipline is essential because without practising mindfulness, meditation, prayer or exercise – without breathwork and getting silent – it is impossible to get the best out of our relationship with ourselves. Our old patterns and limiting beliefs are strong; we need to slow down and replace our former thinking with new ways of being with ourselves.

Changing our daily habits to involve practices that help us to be still and connect to higher parts of ourselves is one of the best ways to do this.

Step 12

SPREADING THE WORD

Spreading the Word

Having had a spiritual awakening because of these steps, we remain vigilant and carry the message wherever we can.

A growing body of evidence indicates that spiritual practices are associated with better health and well-being for many reasons, including Contemplative practice is good for you.

Contemplative practices are activities that guide you to direct your attention to a specific focus—often an inward-looking reflection or concentration on a specific sensation or concept. Many spiritual traditions have a long history of using contemplative practices to increase compassion, empathy, and attention as well as quiet the mind. These qualities will bless your relationships beyond belief.

Because of reading this book, you have been encouraged to engage in many types of contemplative practices. You have experienced a fundamental change in your perception, ideas, attitudes and behaviours. If you have been thorough, your actions will change because of the cognitive change. You have been treated, your whole person, from both inside and out.

"Awakening is not changing who you are but discarding who you are not."

- Deepak Chopra

You are now ready to carry the message to others in the same position and share your experience, strength, and hope.

Ever listened to someone talk about their life and thought, *Oh, someone else has been through that, too, thought it was just me!?* Finding similarities with other people helps us live happy and healthy lives. Your life may feel ordinary to you, but it might seem extraordinary to someone else. Every story shared is a chance to make someone feel less alone.

Today, we still love stories. We love sharing some of our fondest memories as much as we enjoy listening to other people's exciting adventures. We share the best parts of ourselves without realising it. Whether it is a compelling tale of triumph after overcoming adversity or a funny moment that happened to us in passing, storytelling is one of our favourite methods to communicate. It gives us all a greater and more vivid experience of life.

Everyone can get better at creating and sustaining resilience. Almost all of us will experience adversity—most of us will go through some pretty tough times at some point in our lives. Humans have a remarkable capacity to bounce back after problems. Even more impressively, we all have the potential to get even better at resilience.

There is a lot of good advice out there about increasing resilience. I want to focus on the remarkable benefits of sharing your story. Emotional, autobiographical storytelling can be a path to owning your story and taking your power back from the past. Also, by "giving it away," you can use your journey to help others on theirs.

I have been surprised at the power of emotional, autobiographical storytelling. Emotional, autobiographical storytelling means writing about events and people that have mattered to you in your own life—not just describing the facts of your lives.

Research shows that even brief autobiographical storytelling exercises can have substantial impacts on psychological and physical health even months after the storytelling. Although in the dominant Western culture we often use writing to tell stories, I have also seen the power of oral storytelling.

For example, oral storytelling is a major tool in many interventions developed by American Indian healers. Many cultures have long recognised the importance of telling stories. In her powerful book *Women Who Run with the Wolves*, Author and Psychoanalyst Clarissa Pinkola Estes cites West African folklore in which the healers ask the sick, "When was the last time that you sang? When was the last time that you danced? When was the last time that you shared a story?"

So, go out there and tell your story. Talk about what you've experienced, your ups and downs, release it and take control of it, so it no longer festers on the inside of you. And equally important is the fact that you never know whom you might be helping to heal.

I've had my share of life's ups and downs
But fate's been kind, the downs have been few
I guess you could say that I've been lucky
Well, I guess you could say that it's all because of you
If anyone should ever write my life story
For whatever reason there might be
Ooo, you'll be there between each line of pain and glory
'Cause you're the best thing that ever happened to me
Ah, you're the best thing that ever happened to me

7-Day Prayer Challenge

Say a prayer every day this week, either first thing in the morning or last thing at night.

Okay, so if you don't believe in God, it really doesn't matter, just find a prayer that feels right out of the options below or make up your own. It doesn't matter.

The key is to make your spiritual journey work for you, in your way. Just be you having daily conscious contact with your higher power. See if you can start with seven days straight.

Where to start:

You can use the prayers from the Twelve-Step programme as seen in the Big Book of AA—I have used some of them.

Third Step Prayer

God, I offer myself to Thee—to build with me and to do with me as Thou wilt. Relieve me of the bondage of self, that I may better do Thy will. Take away my difficulties, that victory over them may bear witness to those I would help of Thy Power, Thy Love, and Thy Way of life. May I do Thy will always!

Seventh Step Prayer

My Creator, I am now willing that You should have all of me, good and bad. I pray that You now remove from me every single defect of character that stands in the way of my usefulness to You and my fellow man. Grant me strength as I go out from here to do Your bidding.

The Eleventh Step Prayer

Derived from the text found on page 86 of Alcoholics Anonymous—the Big Book: MORNING PRAYER

God, direct my thinking today so that it be empty of self-pity, dishonesty, self-will, self-seeking and fear. God, inspire my thinking, decisions and intuitions. Help me to relax and take it easy. Free me from doubt and indecision. Guide me through this day and show me my next step. God, show me what I need to do to take care of any problems. I ask all these things that I may be of maximum service to You and my fellow man. In the spirit of the Steps I pray. AMEN

Nightly Prayer

God, forgive me for the times when I have been resentful, selfish, dishonest or afraid today. Help me not to keep anything to myself but to discuss it all openly with another person—show me where I owe an apology and help me make it. Help me to be kind and loving to all people. Use me in the mainstream of life, God. Free me of worry, remorse or morbid (sick) reflections that I may be of usefulness to others. AMEN

Prayer of St Francis of Assisi

Lord, make me a channel of Thy peace - that where there is hatred, I may bring love - that where there is wrong, I may bring the spirit of forgiveness - that where there is discord, I may bring harmony - that where there is error, I may bring truth - that where there is doubt, I may bring faith - that where there is despair, I may bring hope - that where there are shadows, I may bring light - that where there is sadness, I may bring joy.

O, Divine Master, grant that I may not so much seek to be consoled, as to console; to be understood as to understand; to be loved, as to love; for it is in the giving that we receive; it is in the pardoning that we are pardoned, and it is in dying that we are born to eternal life.

(Often attributed to St. Francis, from the early 1900s)

Lord, make me an instrument of thy peace.
Where there is hatred, let me sow love;
Where there is injury, pardon;
Where there is doubt, faith;
Where there is despair, hope;
Where there is darkness, light;
Where there is sadness, joy.

O divine Master, grant that I may not so much seek
To be consoled as to console,
To be understood as to understand,
To be loved as to love;
For it is in giving that we receive;
It is in pardoning that we are pardoned;
It is in dying to self that we are born to eternal life.

1. Serenity Prayer

(Short version used in Twelve-Step groups)

God, grant me the serenity to accept the things I cannot change,
The courage to change the things I can,
And wisdom to know the difference.

2. My favourite all-time prayer is Psalm 9,

You can also say this every morning for seven days if you prefer.

Psalm 91

Whoever dwells in the shelter of the Most High
    will rest in the shadow of the Almighty.[a]

I will say of the Lord, "He is my refuge and my fortress,
    my God, in whom I trust."

Surely he will save you
    from the fowler's snare
    and from the deadly pestilence.

He will cover you with his feathers,

and under his wings you will find refuge;
   his faithfulness will be your shield and rampart.

You will not fear the terror of night,
   nor the arrow that flies by day,

nor the pestilence that stalks in the darkness,
   nor the plague that destroys at midday.

A thousand may fall at your side,
   ten thousand at your right hand,
   but it will not come near you

You will only observe with your eyes
   and see the punishment of the wicked.

If you say, "The Lord is my refuge,"
   and you make the Most High your dwelling,

no harm will overtake you,
   no disaster will come near your tent.

For he will command his angels concerning you
   to guard you in all your ways;

they will lift you up in their hands,
   so that you will not strike your foot against a stone.

You will tread on the lion and the cobra;
   you will trample the great lion and the serpent.

"Because he[b] loves me," says the Lord, "I will rescue him;
   I will protect him, for he acknowledges my name

He will call on me, and I will answer him;
   I will be with him in trouble,
   I will deliver him and honor him.

With long life I will satisfy him
   and show him my salvation."

3. If you prefer, just make up your own prayers. Remember, you are just talking to your higher power about everything you feel. Just have a conversation with Him.

Here's a guide I made up to get you started. Just fill in the blanks.

Dear God,

I want to be close to You and to learn how to share all aspects of my life with You. Please give me the willingness to pray every day this week. Please give me the power to overcome all my struggles today and to accept whatever happens in this day with grace and humility—knowing that You are in charge and that all things work for the good of those who stay close to you.

I am feeling _____ today. I think it is because of _____

Can You show me the path I should take today?

And when_____

Please help me to _____

Thank you for calling me back into Your loving presence.

Amen

Reference List

Andriote, J.-M. (2018). You're only as sick as your secrets - Psychology Today. *Psychology Today.* Available at: https://www.psychologytoday.com/ca/blog/stonewall-strong/201803/youre-only-sick-your-secrets [Accessed February 9, 2022].

Albom, M. (2014). *The five people you meet in heaven,* New York: Hachette Books.

Anon, How attachment styles affect adult relationships. *HelpGuide.org.* Available at: https://www.helpguide.org/articles/relationships-communication/attachment-and-adult-relationships.htm [Accessed February 9, 2022].

Chapman, G.D. (2015). *The 5 love languages,* Chicago: Northfield Pub.

Campbell, J., Cousineau, P. & Brown, S.L. (2014). *The hero's journey: Joseph Campbell on his life and work* 3rd., Novato (Calif.): New World Library.

Cameron, J. (2020). *The artist's way: A spiritual path to higher creativity,* London: Souvenir Press.

Chödrön, P. (2002). *The places that scare you: A guide to fearlessness in difficult times,* Boston: Shambhala.

Estés, C.P. (2003). *Women who run with the wolves: Myths and stories of the wild woman archetype,* New York: Ballantine Books.

Fein, E. & Schneider, S. (2000). *Complete book of rules - time tested secrets for capturing the heart of mr. right,* Harpercollins Publishers.

Fielding, H. (2001). *Bridget Jones's diary,* London: Picador.

Freud, S. & Freud, A. (2008). *The Essentials of Psycho-analysis* Reprint., London: Vintage Classics.

Gabrielle, B. (2018). *The Universe has your back: Transform fear to faith,* Carlsbad, CA: Hay House, Inc.

Gerhardt, S. (2015). *Why love matters: How affection shapes a baby's brain,* London: Routledge, Taylor & Francis Group.

Goddard, N. (2019). *Infinite potential: The greatest works of Neville Goddard* M. Horowitz, ed.,

New York: St. Martin's Essentials.

Gray, J. (1992). *Men are from Mars women are from Venus: A practical guide for improving communication and getting what you want in your relationships*, London: Thorsons.

Greenwell, R.D. (2019). *How to wear a crown: a practical guide to knowing your worth*, Independently Published.

Hagerty, B.B. (2009). Prayer may reshape your brain ... and your reality. *NPR*. Available at: https://www.npr.org/templates/story/story.php?storyId=104310443 [Accessed February 9, 2022].

Hale, M. (2013). *The Single Woman: Life, Love, and a dash of sass*, Nashville: Thomas Nelson.

Harvey, S. (2009). *Act like a lady, think like a man*, New York: Harper.

Hendrix, H. (1989). *Getting the love you want: A couples' study guide*, New York: Institute for Relationship Therapy.

Hicks, E. & Hicks, J. (2009). *Vortex - where the law of attraction assembles all cooperative relationship*, Hay House Inc.

Hinshelwood, R.D. (1991). *A dictionary of kleinian thought*, London: Free Association.

hooks, bell (2018). *All about love: New visions*, New York: HarperCollins Publishers.

Jami, C. (2016). *Healology*, CreateSpace Independent Publishing Platform.

Kahn, M. (2003). *Basic freud: Psychoanalytic thought for the Twenty First Century*, New York: BasicBooks.

Katehakis, A., Bliss, T. & Reich, A. (2014). *Mirror of intimacy: Daily Reflections on emotional and Erotic Intelligence*, Los Angeles, CA: Center for Healthy Sex.

Larkin, P., This be the verse by Philip Larkin. *Poetry Foundation*. Available at: https://www.poetryfoundation.org/poems/48419/this-be-the-verse [Accessed February 9, 2022].

Mellody, P., Miller, A.W. & Miller, K. (2003). *Facing codependence: What it is, where it comes from, how it sabotages our lives*, New York: HarperOne.

Miller, A. (1990). *The drama of The gifted child: The search for the true self*, New York: Basic Books.

Newberg, A.B. & Waldman, M.R. (2010). *How god changes your brain: Breakthrough findings from a leading neuroscientist*, New York: Ballantine Books Trade Paperbacks.

Salzberger-Wittenberg, I. (1970). *Psycho-analytic insight and relationships: A Kleinian approach,* Hove, U.K: Brunner-Routledge.

Samuels, A., Shorter, B. & Plaut, F. (1986). *A critical dictionary of Jungian analysis,* London: Routledge.

Thomas, K.W. (2004). *Calling in 'the one': 7 weeks to attract the love of your life,* New York: Harmony Books.

Thomas, K.W. (2016). *Conscious uncoupling: 5 steps to living happily even after,* London: Yellow Kite.

Wolf, S. & Zweig, C. (1997). *Romancing the shadow: A guide to soul work for a vital, authenic life,* New York, NY: Random House Ballantine Publishing.

Woodman, M. & Mellick, J. (2000). *Coming home to myself: Reflections for nurturing A woman's body and Soul,* Berkeley, CA: Conari Press.

Nobus, D. (2018). Psychoanalysis as Poetry in Lacan's Clinical Paradigm*. In A. Mukherjee (Ed.), *After Lacan: Literature, Theory and Psychoanalysis in the Twenty-First Century* (After Series, pp. 74-92). Cambridge: Cambridge University Press. doi:10.1017/9781108650311.005